I0683419

THE HOLY SPIRIT of God

THE HOLY SPIRIT

of God

BY:

MICHAEL STEVEN KENWORTHEY

ARPress
ILLUMINATING IDEAS
EMPOWERING VOICES

Copyright © 2024 by Michael Steven Kenworthey

All rights reserved solely by the author. No part of this publication may be reproduced, distributed, or transmitted in any form or by any means, including photocopying, recording, or other electronic or mechanical methods, without the prior written permission of the author, the copyright owner, except in the case of brief quotations embodied in critical reviews and certain other noncommercial uses permitted by copyright law. For permission requests, write to the publisher, addressed "Attention: Permissions Coordinator," at the address below.

Unless otherwise indicated, Scripture quotations taken from The Holy Bible, the King James Version (KJV) – *public domain.*

The New Strong's Exhaustive Concordance of the Bible King James Version Copyright © 1995, 1996 by Thomas Nelson Publishers

An American Dictionary of the English Language, Noah Webster 1828 Facsimile, First Edition. Permission to reprint the 1828 edition granted by G. & C. Merriam Company. Copyright © 1967 & 1995 (Renewal) by Rosalie J. Slater. Published by the Foundation for American Christian Education, Chesapeake, VA.

Author: Michael Steven Kenworthey

> **The Ministry of 2 Timothy 3:16,17**

> **https://www.theministryof2timothy3.com**

ARPress
45 Dan Road Suite 5
Canton MA 02021

Hotline:	1(888) 821-0229
Fax:	1(508) 545-7580

Ordering Information:

Quantity sales. Special discounts are available on quantity purchases by corporations, associations, and others. For details, contact the publisher at the address above.

Printed in the United States of America.

ISBN-13:	Softcover	979-8-89330-382-7
	Hardcover	979-8-89356-211-8

Library of Congress Control Number: 2024902883

I dedicate this book to:

the **Creator**

my Creator

Genesis 1:1

In the beginning God created the heaven and the earth.

1Peter 4:19

Wherefore let them that suffer according to the will of God commit the keeping of their souls *to him* in well doing, as unto a faithful Creator.

Revelation 4:11

Thou art worthy, O Lord, to receive glory and honour and power: for thou hast created all things, and for thy pleasure they are and were created.

the **Father**

my Father

Matthew 6:9-13

9 After this manner therefore pray ye: Our Father which art in heaven, Hallowed be thy name.
10 Thy kingdom come. Thy will be done in earth, as *it is* in heaven. 11 Give us this day our daily bread.
12 And forgive us our debts, as we forgive our debtors. 13 And lead us not into temptation, but deliver us from evil:
For thine is the kingdom, and the power, and the glory, for ever. A-men'.

John 16:27

For the Father himself loveth you, because ye have loved me, and have believed that I came out from God.

the **Son,**

Jesus Christ

my Lord & my Saviour

John 14:6

Jesus saith unto him, I am the way, the truth, and the life: no man cometh unto the Father, but by me.

John 1:14

And the Word was made flesh, and dwelt among us, (and we beheld his glory, the glory as of the only begotten of the Father,) full of grace and truth.

1John 5:20

And we know that the Son of God is come, and hath given us an understanding, that we may know him that is true, and we are in him that is true, *even* in his Son Jesus Christ.

Acts 4:10-12

10 Be it known unto you all, and to all the people of Israel, that by the name of Jesus Christ of Nazareth, whom ye crucified, whom God raised from the dead, *even* by him doth this man stand here before you whole. 11 This is the stone which was set at nought of you builders, which is become the head of the corner. 12 Neither is there salvation in any other: for there is none other name under heaven given among men, whereby we must be saved.

the **Holy Spirit** / the **Comforter**

my Comforter

John 14:26

But the Comforter, *which is* the Holy Ghost, whom the Father will send in my name, he shall teach you all things, and bring all things to your remembrance, whatsoever I have said unto you.

John 15:26

But when the Comforter is come, whom I will send unto you from the Father, *even* the Spirit of truth, which proceedeth from the Father, he shall testify of me:

1John 5:7

For there are three that bear record in heaven, the Father, the Word, and the Holy Ghost: and these three are one.

<u>Almighty God</u>

my God
who is holy and true:

1Thessalonians 1:9

For they themselves shew of us what manner of entering in we had unto you, and how ye turned to God from idols to serve the living and true God;

10 And to wait for his Son from heaven, whom he raised from the dead, *even* Jesus, which delivered us from the wrath to come.

1John 5:20

And we know that the Son of God is come, and hath given us an understanding, that we may know him that is true, and we are in him that is true, *even* in his Son Jesus Christ. This is the true God, and eternal life.

Revelation 4:8

And the four beasts had each of them six wings about *him*; and *they were* full of eyes within: and they rest not day and night, saying, Holy, holy, holy, Lord God Almighty, which was, and is, and is to come.

Revelation 6:10

And they cried with a loud voice, saying, How long, O Lord, holy and true, dost thou not judge and avenge our blood on them that dwell on the earth?

HIS word endures for ever!

1Peter 1:25

But the word of the Lord endureth for ever.
And this is the word which by the gospel is preached unto you.

Even so, come, Lord Jesus. ***Revelation 22:20*** *vs.21* … A-men'.

7

To a witness of the Lord Jesus Christ:

This book of the Holy Spirit is to help ground a mature believer in the truth of God's word and it is to help a mature believer become a greater witness for his Lord, according to God's holy word; which was written by the inspiration of the Holy Spirit and by true servants of the Lord; preserving HIS word for our edification and for the increasing of one's intimate Faith in Almighty God!!!

2Timothy 3:16 All scripture is given by inspiration of God, and is profitable for doctrine, for reproof, for correction, for instruction in righteousness: **17** That the man of God may be perfect, throughly furnished unto all good works.

Revelation 1:9 I John, who also am your brother, and companion in tribulation, and in the kingdom and patience of Jesus Christ, was in the isle that is called Patmos, for the word of God, and for the testimony of Jesus Christ. **10** I was in the Spirit on the Lord's day, and heard behind me a great voice, as of a trumpet. **11** Saying, I am Alpha and Omega, the first and the last: and, What thou seest, write in a book, and send it unto the seven churches which are in Asia;

I thank you Lord God Almighty for preserving your WORD, now and for ever! and I thank you Lord Jesus: You are the Word of God and the Saviour of the world!!!
Now and For Ever!

To all who read this book:

I encourage you to be a true and faithful witness of God; leading a person to accept the Lord Jesus Christ, as one's own personal Lord & Saviour; according to the Lord's written word: Which is absolute truth!

Revelation 22:17
And the Spirit and the bride say, Come. And let him that heareth say, Come.
And let him that is athirst come. And whosoever will, let him take the water of life freely.

Even so, come, Lord Jesus. *Revelation 22:20* *vs. 21* … A-men'.

Recorded by:
Michael Steven Kenworthey
a servant of the one true God!
Now & For Ever!
A-men'.

Revelation 22:21
The grace of our Lord Jesus Christ *be* with you all. A-men'.

Heavenly Father
prayer

Heavenly Father, LORD, I come before you and I do thank you, and I do praise your name,

₁₀ That at the name of Jesus every knee should bow, of *things* in heaven, and *things* in earth, and *things* under the earth;   ₁₁ And *that* every tongue should confess that Jesus Christ *is* Lord, to the glory of God the Father. **Philippians 2:10,11**

Psalm 46:10 Be still, and know that I *am* God:

You are God and you are Lord and you are SAVIOUR !

You are: Alpha and Omega, the beginning and the end, the first and the last.   *Revelation 22:13*

the bright and morning star.   *Revelation 22:16*

Revelation 22:13 & 16

John 10:10   *In you I have life and I have life more abundantly.*

Romans 8:16,17 The Spirit itself beareth witness with our spirit, that we are the children of God: ₁₇ And if children, then heirs; heirs of God, and joint-heirs with Christ; if so be that we suffer with *him*, that we may be also glorified together.

Philippians 4:7 And the peace of God, which passeth all understanding,
                              shall keep your hearts and minds through Christ Jesus.

Hebrews 11:1 *and* **2**

₁ Now faith is the substance of things hoped for, the evidence of things not seen.

₂ For by it the elders obtained a good report.

And I do acknowledge Jesus as my personal LORD and SAVIOUR.

And I do pray this in His, <u>*holy*</u> *and* <u>*precious*</u> *name.*

A-men' unto the Father, my Father, whereby I cry, Abba, Father !

A-men' unto the Son, my Lord and my Saviour Jesus Christ, in whom I am saved; now and for ever !

A-men' unto the Holy Spirit of God, my Comforter, in whom I am comforted and I am sealed;
                              unto the day of redemption !

Even so, come, Lord Jesus. **Revelation 22:20**   *vs. 21* … A-men' .

The Holy Spirit

Luke 1:15 For he shall be great in the sight of the Lord, and shall drink neither wine nor strong drink; and he shall be filled with the Holy Ghost, even from his mother's womb.

My note: John the Baptist was filled with the Holy Ghost from his mother's womb. He didn't have to seek for the filling of the Holy Ghost.

John 3:30 He must increase, but I *must* decrease.   *My note: John's ministry decreased while he was filled with the Holy Ghost.*

Luke 3:20 Added yet this above all, that he shut up John in prison.

My note: Herod shut John up in prison while John was Spirit filled.

My note: he = Herod

Matthew 14:10 And he sent, and beheaded John in the prison.   *My note: John was beheaded while Spirit filled.*

John 10:40-42 40 And went away again beyond Jordan into the place where John at first baptized; and there he abode. 41 And many resorted unto him, and said, John did no miracle: but all things that John spake of this man were true. 42 And many believed on him there.

Jesus did many miracles

John 11:11 These things said he: and after that he saith unto them, **Our friend Lazarus sleepeth; but I go, that I may awake him out of sleep.**
Read: 11:1 - 48

Romans 3:10 As it is written, There is none righteous, no, not one:

Romans 3:11 There is none that understandeth, there is none that seeketh after God.

Romans 3:12 They are all gone out of the way, they are together become unprofitable; there is none that doeth good, no, not one.

My note: There is no reference in the KingJamesVersion of the Holy Bible, for a man to seek for the Holy Ghost to fill you ; for one to ask to receive the Holy Spirit ; for one to desire to be filled with the Holy Ghost in order to perform signs and wonders, as was given in the day of Pentecost .

Romans 8:9 But ye are not in the flesh, but in the Spirit, if so be that the Spirit of God dwell in you. Now if any man have not the Spirit of Christ, he is none of his.

John 3:8 **The wind bloweth where it listeth, and thou hearest the sound thereof, but canst not tell whence it cometh, and whither it goeth: so is every one that is born of the Spirit.**

My note: This word is from Jesus to Nicodemus, an unbeliever; A child of God knows, whence and whither!

2Corinthians 11:4 For if he that cometh preacheth another Jesus, whom we have not preached, or *if* ye receive another spirit, which ye have not received, or another gospel, which ye have not accepted, ye might well bear with *him*.

Matthew 10:8 **Heal the sick, cleanse the lepers, raise the dead, cast out devils: freely ye have received, freely give.**
Read: 9:35 – 11:1
My note: This scripture is specifically for the twelve disciples of Jesus.

The Holy Spirit
continued...

The focus of John's ministry is Christ.
The focus of a person's life should be Jesus Christ.
The Holy Spirit glorifies the Father and the Lord Jesus Christ.

Luke 1:15   *Fill*, v.t. *To occupy*   **Filled**, pp. *Made full ; to supply with abundance.*

Matthew 14:1-13 ; Mark 6:16,27

Jesus did many miracles

John 21:25 And there are also many other things which Jesus did, the which, if they should be written every one, I suppose that even the world itself could not contain the books that should be written. A-men'.

Romans 3:11   *My note: The Holy Spirit seeks the lost, mostly through others: <u>preaching</u>, <u>teaching</u>, <u>sharing</u>.*
My note: If a man doesn't have the Holy Ghost, he is not saved.
My note: When a man receives Jesus Christ as his personal Lord and Savior,
he receives the Holy Ghost.

Romans 8:9 ; 1Corinthians 3:16 ; 1John 4:13 ;

*<u>My note</u>: <u>**The Holy Spirit dwells in every believer, if not, you are not born again; you are not a child of God;**</u>*
*<u>**you are not a believer!**</u>*

John 3:8   *List*, v.i. *Properly, to lean or incline; to be propense; hence, to desire or choose.*
Whence, adv. 1. *From what place*
Whither, adv. 2. *To what place, absolutely.*

My note: A lost person cannot understand a person who is born again. He, the lost person, cannot tell from what place the person who is born again, has come from or what place he is going. (spiritually speaking)
To the person who is lost: There is something very different and somewhat confusing about this truth.
So, we are to recognize who we are speaking to and declare Scripture, according to the leading of the Holy Spirit.

2Corinthians 11:4   ye might *(of ignorance) ;* ye might *= I do not know*

May, verb aux. ; pret. might. 1. *To be possible.*
Might, pret. of may. 2. *It sometimes denotes was possible, <u>implying ignorance of the fact in the speaker.</u>*
well *(favorably)*
bear with *(remain with)*   **11:1** bear with *= to remain with him*

2Corinthians 11:3,4,5
11:4 ye might well bear with *him.* *= I do not know if you will favorably remain with him.*

<u>These verses go together and connect with each other for true understanding</u>.

11:3 But I fear, lest by any means, as the serpent beguiled Eve through his subtilty,
so your minds should be corrupted from the simplicity that is in Christ.
11:4 For if he that cometh preacheth another Jesus, whom we have not preached, or *if* ye receive another spirit, which ye have not received, or another gospel, which ye have not accepted,
ye might well bear with *him.*
11:13 For such *are* false apostles, deceitful workers, transforming themselves into the apostles of Christ.
*<u>My note</u>: **A person <u>can receive another spirit</u> or <u>accept another gospel.</u>***

Hold fast to these two truths! **The Spirit of God** *; who is* **the Holy Spirit** *and*
the word of God *; which is God's holy word written down:* **the Holy Bible.**

Romans 8:16,17   16 The Spirit itself beareth witness with our spirit, that we are the children of God:
17 And if children, then heirs; heirs of God, and joint-heirs with Christ;
if so be that we suffer with *him*, that we may be also glorified together.

Romans 10:17 So then faith *cometh* by hearing, and hearing by the word of God.
Read: 10:8 - 17

Ephesians 6:17 And take the helmet of salvation, and the sword of the Spirit, which is the word of God:

My note: helmet of salvation   *is*   *knowing God's holy word* *unto salvation*   and   the sword of the Spirit   *is God's holy word.*
My note: *The Holy Bible is the sword of the Spirit. A sword is used for offence; God's holy word penetrates the heart.*

1Thessalonians 2:13   For this cause also thank we God without ceasing, because, when ye received the word
of God which ye heard of us, ye received *it* not *as* the word of men, but as it is in truth,
the word of God, which effectually worketh also in you that believe.

2Timothy 2:15 Study to shew thyself approved unto God, a workman that needeth not to be ashamed,
rightly dividing the word of truth.

2Timothy 3:16 All scripture *is* given by inspiration of God, and *is* profitable for doctrine, for reproof,
for correction, for instruction in righteousness: 17 That the man of God may be perfect,
throughly furnished unto all good works.

2Timothy 4:2 Preach the word; be instant in season, out of season;
reprove, rebuke, exhort with all longsuffering and doctrine.

Personality and description of the Holy Spirit

The Holy Spirit is holy:
He is pure; He is forever holy; He is unchanging.

Psalm 51:11 Cast me not away from thy presence; and take not thy holy spirit from me.
Romans 1:4 And declared *to be* the Son of God with power, according to the spirit of holiness,
by the resurrection from the dead:
Hebrews 13:8 Jesus Christ the same yesterday, and to day, and for ever.
Malachi 3:6 For I *am* the LORD, I change not; therefore ye sons of Jacob are not consumed.

My note:
Even though God doesn't change, HE deals with mankind differently in different ages.

For example:
Old Testament men brought animals to God to sacrifice, for a sin offering. Today no one brings blood sacrifices to God as a sin offering because man, who is a sinner, must trust in the finished work of the Lord Jesus Christ on the Cross at Calvary; HE paid the sin debt in full, in order to have sin removed.
2Corinthians 5:21 For he hath made him *to be* sin for us, who knew no sin;
that we might be made the righteousness of God in him.

Before the resurrection of Jesus Christ, men could ask for the Holy Ghost?

Luke 11:13 **If ye then, being evil, know how to give good gifts unto your children:**
how much more shall *your* heavenly Father give the Holy Spirit to them that ask him?

This is another direct reference to Jesus empowering his disciples to do the work set before them prior to HIS death, burial, and resurrection and prior to the day of Pentecost; where HIS disciples received the Holy Ghost, the Comforter, that Jesus promised to send after HIS death, burial, and resurrection. This is also based on them having faith in Jesus Christ as HE walked and talked and taught them.

My note: Jesus is establishing HIS authority and HE is teaching HIS disciples a lesson in trusting the Father and trusting HIM; the ONE sent by the Father to save the world!

My note: HE is pure, in and of HIMSELF; **Exodus 3:14** I AM THAT I AM ; *HE is perfect, in and of HIMSELF!*

> *Holy, a. 1. Properly, whole, entire or perfect ... Applied to the Supreme Being, holy signifies perfectly pure,*
>
> *Perfect, a. 1. Finished; complete*

Before the resurrection of Jesus Christ

My note: The first sacrifice was made by the LORD to clothe or cover over Adam and Eve's sin, so that HE could still have a relationship with them. No doubt it was a lamb which was slain because, the LORD accepted Abel's offering, "the firstlings of his flock and the fat thereof." and HE rejected Cain's offering.

Genesis 3:21 Unto Adam also and to his wife did the LORD God make coats of skins, and clothed them.

Genesis 4:3-5   3 And in process of time it came to pass, that Cain brought of the fruit of the ground an offering unto the LORD. 4 And Abel, he also brought of the firstlings of his flock and of the fat thereof. And the LORD had respect unto Abel and to his offering: 5 But unto Cain and to his offering he had not respect. And Cain was wroth, and his countenance fell.

1Corinthians 15:21,22   21 For since by man *came* death, by man *came* also the resurrection of the dead. 22 For as in Adam all die, even so in Christ shall all be made alive.

For example:

The sacrificial system
The LORD → to → Adam
Adam → to → Cain and Abel
Adam → to → Seth
Seth → to → and so on →
ending with **THE LORD JESUS CHRIST**

John 1:29 The next day John seeth Jesus coming unto him, and saith, Behold the Lamb of God, which taketh away the sin of the world.

Jesus Christ is the end of the sacrificial system of the LORD, FOREVER.

Hebrews 9:24–28 24 For Christ is not entered into the holy places made with hands, *which are* the figures of the true; but into heaven itself, now to appear in the presence of God for us: 25 Nor yet that he should offer himself often, as the high priest entereth into the holy place every year with blood of others; 26 For then must he often have suffered since the foundation of the world: but now once in the end of the world hath he appeared to put away sin by the sacrifice of himself. 27 And as it is appointed unto men once to die, but after this the judgment: 28 So Christ was once offered to bear the sins of many; and unto them that look for him shall he appear the second time without sin unto salvation.

Hebrews 10:12-18 12 But this man, after he had offered one sacrifice for sins for ever, sat down on the right hand of God; 13 From henceforth expecting till his enemies be made his footstool. 14 For by one offering he hath perfected for ever them that are sanctified. 15 *Whereof* the Holy Ghost also is a witness to us: for after that he had said before, 16 This *is* the covenant that I will make with them after those days, saith the Lord, I will put my laws into their hearts, and in their minds will I write them; 17 And their sins and iniquities will I remember no more. 18 Now where remission of these *is*, *there is* no more offering for sin.

Ephesians 5:2 And walk in love, as Christ also hath loved us, and hath given himself for us an offering and a sacrifice to God for a sweetsmelling savour.

The Holy Spirit is good

Psalm 143:10   Teach me to do thy will; for thou *art* my God: thy spirit *is* good;
lead me into the land of uprightness.

Nehemiah 9:20 Thou gavest also thy good spirit to instruct them, and withheldest not thy manna from their mouth,
and gavest them water for their thirst.

Matthew 19:17 And he said unto him, **Why callest thou me good?** *there is* **none good but one,** *that is,* **God:
but if thou wilt enter into life, keep the commandments.**

Ephesians 2:2 Wherein in time past ye walked according to the course of this world,
according to the prince of the power of the air, the spirit that now
worketh in the children of disobedience:

*Side note: There is another spirit that works in (inside) the children of disobedience.
This could be one's own spirit being influenced by the prince of the power of
the air, the devil. Prior to being born again we had this other spirit doing
work within us; Without the Holy Spirit dwelling within us, we continually
yielded unto this other spirit.*

Ephesians 6:12 For we wrestle not against flesh and blood, but against principalities,
against powers, against the rulers of the darkness of this world,
against spiritual wickedness in high *places*.

The Holy Spirit is the Spirit of God

Genesis 1:1 In the beginning God created the heaven and the earth.
Genesis 1:2 And the earth was without form, and void; and darkness *was* upon the face of the deep.
And the Spirit of God moved upon the face of the waters.

1Corinthians 3:16   Know ye not that ye are the temple of God, and *that* the Spirit of God dwelleth in you?

*Side note: There is no such thing as a holy church building; God does not dwell in buildings;
He dwells within the believer.*

Ephesians 4:30   And grieve not the holy Spirit of God, whereby ye are sealed unto the day of redemption.

The Holy Spirit is the Comforter

John 14:16,17   16 **And I will pray the Father, and he shall give you another Comforter, that he may abide
with you for ever;** 17 *Even* **the Spirit of truth; whom the world cannot receive,
because it seeth him not, neither knoweth him: but ye know him;
for he dwelleth with you, and shall be in you.**

John 14:26 **But the Comforter,** *which is* **the Holy Ghost, whom the Father will send in my name, he shall
teach you all things, and bring all things to your remembrance, whatsoever I have said unto you.**

Acts 2:1-8 4 And they were all filled with the Holy Ghost, and began to speak with other tongues,
as the Spirit gave them utterance.
8 And how hear we every man in our own tongue, wherein we were born?

The Holy Spirit is the Spirit of God and the Spirit of Christ

Romans 8:9 But ye are not in the flesh, but in the Spirit, if so be that the Spirit of God dwell in you.
Now if any man have not the Spirit of Christ, he is none of his.

*Side note: The Spirit of God and the Spirit of Christ are the same; THEY are ONE.
Everyone who is born again has the Spirit of Christ living within him; The Holy Spirit dwelling within him !*

The Holy Spirit is the Spirit of grace

Hebrews 10:29 Of how much sorer punishment, suppose ye, shall he be thought worthy, who hath trodden under
foot the Son of God, and hath counted the blood of the covenant, wherewith he was sanctified,
an unholy thing, and hath done despite unto the Spirit of grace?

1Corinthians 3:16 Know ye not that <u>ye are the temple of God</u>, and *that* <u>the Spirit of God dwelleth in you</u>?

Ephesians 4:30 And grieve not the holy Spirit of God, whereby <u>ye are</u> sealed unto the day of redemption.

Ephesians 4:30   the day of redemption
                         /\
Redemption happens at <u>a set time</u>, when our body is redeemed / glorified!

My note:
Guilt is a great bondage of sin. Christ's act of atonement removed all guilt of offending the
holiness of God! All who receive Jesus Christ as his own personal LORD and SAVIOUR becomes
a new creature. One without guilt! Yet, the Holy Spirit can be grieved with one's own mindset;
                                                    and with one's actions!

<u>**Grieve**</u>, *v.t. To offend; to displease; to provoke.*   *Grieve not the holy Spirit of God.* **Eph. iv**.

<u>**Sealed**</u> *- unalterable; definite; absolute*

<u>**Unto**</u> *- moving toward and continually affirming*
Un = On - <u>continuance; without ceasing or interruption</u>
To - toward; <u>affirmation</u> (<u>guarantee; definite</u>)

<u>**Redeem**</u>, *v.t. [L. redimo red, re, and emo, <u>to obtain or purchase.</u>]*
1. To purchase back; to ransom; to liberate or rescue from captivity or bondage, by paying an equivalent.
5. To free by making <u>atonement</u>.
7. To save.
10. In theology, to rescue and deliver from the bondage of sin and the penalties of God's violated law,
*   by obedience and suffering in the place of the sinner, or by doing and suffering that which is*
*   accepted in <u>lieu</u> of the sinner's obedience.* **Galatians iii** . ; **Titus ii** .

      <u>**Lieu**</u>, *n. Place ; room ; <u>stead</u>*   **Stead**, *n. 2. Place or room which another had or might have,*
                                       noting substitution, replacing or filling the place of another;

<u>**Redemption**</u>, *n. 6. In theology, the purchase of God's favor by the death and sufferings of Christ;*
                  the ransom or deliverance of sinners from the bondage of sin and the penalties
                  of God' s violated law by the <u>atonement</u> of Christ. Dryden . Nelson .   **Eph. 1:7** ; **Col. 1:14**

    <u>**Atone**</u>, *v.t.   1. To Expiate; to answer or make satisfaction for.*
    <u>**Atonement**</u>, *n. 3. In theology, the <u>expiation</u> of sin made by the obedience and*
                                      personal sufferings of Christ.

        <u>**Expiation**</u>, *n. 1. The act of making satisfaction for an offense, by which the guilt is*
                   done away, and the obligation of the offended person to punish
                               the crime is cancelled.

My note: The sin debt is paid for by the Lord Jesus Christ, which satisfies the holiness of God and removes our guilt.

Philippians 4:7 And <u>the peace of God</u>, which passeth all understanding,
                         shall keep your hearts and minds through Christ Jesus.

The Holy Spirit is the Spirit of truth

John 14:17   *Even* the Spirit of truth; whom the world cannot receive, because it seeth him not,
neither knoweth him: but ye know him; for he dwelleth with you, and shall be in you.

John 16:13   Howbeit when he, the Spirit of truth, is come, he will guide you into all truth: for he shall not
speak of himself; but whatsoever he shall hear, *that* shall he speak: and he will shew you
things to come.

John 15:26   But when the Comforter is come, whom I will send unto you from the Father,
even the Spirit of truth, which proceedeth from the Father, he shall testify of me:

The Holy Spirit is the holy Spirit of promise

Ephesian 1:13,14   13 In whom ye also *trusted*, after that ye heard the word of truth, the gospel of your salvation:
in whom also after that ye believed, ye were sealed with that holy Spirit of promise,
14 Which is the earnest of our inheritance until the redemption of the purchased possession,
unto the praise of his glory.

My note: "the purchased possession" *is the body.*

1Corinthians 12:13,14   13 For by one Spirit are we all baptized into one body, whether *we be* Jews or Gentiles,
whether *we be* bond or free; and have been all made to drink into one Spirit.
14 For the body is not one member, but many.

John 6:47   Verily, verily, I say unto you, He that believeth on me hath everlasting life.   **Philippians 2:12**

The Holy Spirit is the spirit of glory

My note: "the spirit of glory"; "spirit" *is a name which describes the Holy Spirit ; it is not capitalized as a proper noun.*

1Peter 4:14   If ye be reproached for the name of Christ, happy *are ye*; for the spirit of glory and of God resteth
upon you: on their part he is evil spoken of, but on your part he is glorified.

Glorified, pp. *Honored; dignified; exalted to glory.*
Glorify, v.t. *1. To praise; to magnify and honor in worship; to ascribe honor to, in thought or words.*
Glorifying, ppr. *Praising; honoring in worship; exalting to glory; honoring; extolling.*

Verses of encouragement

1Corinthians 15:47 – 58   47 The first man *is* of the earth, earthy: the second man *is* the Lord
from heaven. 48 As *is* the earthy, such *are* they also that are earthy: and as *is* the heavenly, such
are they also that are heavenly. 49 And as we have borne the image of the earthy, we shall also
bear the image of the heavenly. 50 Now this I say, brethren, that flesh and blood cannot inherit
the kingdom of God; neither doth corruption inherit incorruption. 51 Behold, I shew you a mystery;
We shall not all sleep, but we shall all be changed, 52 In a moment, in the twinkling of an eye,
at the last trump: for the trumpet shall sound, and the dead shall be raised incorruptible, and we
shall be changed. 53 For this corruptible must put on incorruption, and this mortal *must* put on
immortality. 54 So when this corruptible shall have put on incorruption, and this mortal shall
have put on immortality, then shall be brought to pass the saying that is written, Death is
swallowed up in victory. 55 O death, where *is* thy sting? O grave, where *is* thy victory? 56 The
sting of death *is* sin; and the strength of sin *is* the law. 57 But thanks *be* to God, which giveth us
the victory through our Lord Jesus Christ. 58 Therefore, my beloved brethren, be ye stedfast,
unmovable, always abounding in the work of the Lord, forasmuch as ye know that your labour
is not in vain in the Lord.

My note: *These are things given to us by God, in and through the Lord Jesus Christ and are guaranteed by the Holy Spirit.*

Ephesians 1:13   The *Sealing* is unalterable
The *Earnest* is the guarantee
Unto is continually affirming

My note: **Having the Holy Spirit dwelling within us is the promise or the guarantee, that our body shall be redeemed and glorified; continually affirming with praise, HIS glory. God receives continual praise for redeeming and saving our body;**   2Corinthians 1:21,22

My note: *Along with our body, HE also saves our soul and spirit from the eternal torment to come ;*
being cast into the lake of fire and brimstone. **Revelation 21:7,8**

Romans 8:23 And not only *they*, but ourselves also, which have the firstfruits of the Spirit,
even we ourselves groan within ourselves, waiting for the adoption, *to wit,*
the redemption of our body.

My note: *The redemption of our body is very important to a Christian! and also, to those who are lost and walking according to this world; there grows a weariness, despair, etc., upon all men. Sin does have a stronghold! But we who are saved, have a hope which is stronger than the present weariness of this world!*

1Corinthians 12:13   "one body" *is in Christ. All believers are one in Christ and are baptized into Christ by the Holy Spirit and all to the glory of God the Father.*

Made, pret. and pp. of *make*.
Make, v.t. [... The primary sense is ... to press, drive, strain or compel,
as in the phrases, make your servant work, make him go.]

Drink, v.t. 3. To take in by any inlet; *To drink in*, to absorb; to take or receive into any inlet.
My note: Individually in mind & heart, in spirit, we absorb " into one Spirit "; *being one in the Spirit.*
My note: Individually being compelled in spirit, we come together " into one Spirit " *and unite as one in the Spirit.*

Into, prep, 6. *Noting the passing of a thing from one form or state to another.*
My note: To pass from a mind without unity of the Spirit into a spirit of unity, in the Holy Spirit.

Hebrews 10:21-23   21 And *having* an high priest over the house of God; 22 Let us draw near with a true heart in full assurance of faith, having our hearts sprinkled from an evil conscience, and our bodies washed with pure water. 23 Let us hold fast the profession of *our* faith without wavering;
(for he *is* faithful that promised;)

My note: The moment that one believes unto salvation he receives the promise of everlasting life, being with the Lord in heaven; the promise of eternal life is sealed by the Holy Spirit. The question is, at what moment in time does a person truly believe in his heart and truly confess with his mouth? **Romans 10:10**

John 6:47   **Philippians 2:5-13**   12 Wherefore, my beloved, as ye have always obeyed, not as in my presence only, but now much more in my absence, work out your own salvation with fear and trembling.
Ephesians 4:30 And grieve not the holy Spirit of God, whereby ye are sealed unto the day of redemption.

The Holy Spirit is the spirit of glory continued. ...

1Peter 4:14   "on their part" *of them ;* "he" *Christ ;* "is evil spoken of" ;
"but" ; "on your part" *of you ;* "he" *Christ ;* "is glorified" *lifted up in your heart*

1Peter 4:1 – 14 *go together*
"the Gentiles" **1Peter 4:3**
1Peter 4:4 *is a direct reference to* **4:14**
"on their part" "the Gentiles" **1Peter 4:4,12,14**
"of them" "the Gentiles" **4:4,12,14** ; "he" *Christ* "is evil spoken of"
"but"

"on your part" *of you ;* "he is glorified" *of you Christ is glorified! ; of you* = "the strangers" "Elect"

1:1,2   1 PETER, an apostle of Jesus Christ, to the strangers scattered throughout Pontus, Galatia, Cappadocia, Asia, Bithynia, 2 Elect according to the foreknowledge of God the Father, through sanctification of the Spirit, unto obedience and sprinkling of the blood of Jesus Christ: Grace unto you, and peace, be multiplied.

4:10,11   10 As every man hath received the gift, *even so* minister the same one to another, as good stewards of the manifold grace of God. 11 If any man speak, *let him speak* as the oracles of God; if any man minister, *let him do it* as of the ability which God giveth: that God in all things may be glorified through Jesus Christ, to whom be praise and dominion for ever and ever. A-men'.

The relationship of the Holy Spirit
Relationships to other persons indicate personality

Acts 15:28   For it seemed good to the Holy Ghost, and to us, to lay upon you no greater burden than these necessary things;

John 16:14   13 Howbeit when he, the Spirit of truth, is come, he will guide you into all truth: for he shall not speak of himself; but whatsoever he shall hear, *that* shall he speak: and he will shew you things to come. 14 He shall glorify me: for he shall receive of mine, and shall shew *it* unto you. 15 All things that the Father hath are mine: therefore said I, that he shall take of mine, and shall shew *it* unto you.

Matthew 28:18,19   18 And Jesus came and spake unto them, saying, All power is given unto me in heaven and in earth. 19 Go ye therefore, and teach all nations, baptizing them in the name of the Father, and of the Son, and of the Holy Ghost:

My note: (*The Holy Ghost* is equated here with *the Father* and *the Son; declaring the oneness of Almighty God !*)

Luke 1:35   And the angel answered and said unto her, The Holy Ghost shall come upon thee, and the power of the Highest shall overshadow thee: therefore also that holy thing which shall be born of thee shall be called the Son of God.

My note: The person of the Holy Ghost is the power of the Highest.

Luke 4:14   And Jesus returned in the power of the Spirit into Galilee: and there went out a fame of him through all the region round about.

Romans 15:13   Now the God of hope fill you with all joy and peace in believing, that ye may abound in hope, through the power of the Holy Ghost.

The Holy Spirit's actions indicate personality

The Holy Spirit teaches

John 14:26   But the Comforter, *which is* the Holy Ghost, whom the Father will send in my name, he shall teach you all things, and bring all things to your remembrance, whatsoever I have said unto you.

My note: This is how these people wrote down the events of walking with Jesus after HIS death, burial, and resurrection. Only a person can teach, an influence cannot teach.

The Holy Spirit testifies

John 15:26   But when the Comforter is come, whom I will send unto you from the Father, *even* the Spirit of truth, which proceedeth from the Father, he shall testify of me:

Romans 8:16   The Spirit itself beareth witness with our spirit, that we are the children of God:

The Holy Spirit guides

Romans 8:14   For as many as are led by the Spirit of God, they are the sons of God.

John 16:13   Howbeit when he, the Spirit of truth, is come, he will guide you into all truth: for he shall not speak of himself; but whatsoever he shall hear, *that* shall he speak: and he will shew you things to come.

The Holy Spirit calls or sends

Acts 13:2-5   2 As they ministered to the Lord, and fasted, the Holy Spirit said, Separate me Barnabas and Saul for the work whereunto I have called them. 3 And when they had fasted and prayed, and laid *their* hands on them, they sent *them* away. 4 So they, being sent forth by the Holy Ghost, departed unto Seleucia; and from thence they sailed to Cyprus. 5 And when they were at Salamis, they preached the word of God in the synagogues of the Jews: and they had also John to *their* minister.

The Holy Spirit's actions indicate personality
continued ...

The Holy Spirit teaches

My own personal testimony of the Comforter teaching me, and testifying to me, and guiding me!

After my automobile accident in 2009, the Lord gave me in my memory these Scriptural verses,
which I had never before memorized:

My note:
The words which are in quotes are the words which HE gave to me in my memory.

"Be still and know that I am God"

Psalm 46:10
Be still, and know that I *am* God:

"That at the name of Jesus every knee should bow, of things in heaven and things in the earth and things under the
earth, and that every tongue should confess that Jesus Christ is Lord, to the glory of God the Father."

Philippians 2:10,11
10 That at the name of Jesus every knee should bow, of *things* in heaven, and *things* in earth, and *things* under the
earth; 11 And *that* every tongue should confess that Jesus Christ *is* Lord, to the glory of God the Father.

"The Spirit beareth witness with my spirit that I am His."

The above quote is not a distortion of Scripture, but was personalized for me at that time.

Romans 8:16
The Spirit itself beareth witness with our spirit, that we are the children of God:

I had to reference these Scriptural verses in order to know where they are located within the Holy Scriptures.

The Holy Spirit testifies

Proceed, *v.i.*   *3. To issue or come as from a source or fountain. Light proceeds form the sun;*
4. To come from a person or place. Christ says, "I proceeded forth and came from God." **John viii**.

Proceedeth – *to come forth*   *3. To issue or come, as a source or fountain*   *4. To come from a person; to flow out.*

The Holy Spirit calls and sends

(Barnabas and Saul)
My note: *The Holy Spirit called and separated out and sent* <u>them</u> *forth to preach the word of God in the synagogues*
of the Jews:

<u>*My calling and my being sent*</u> : *The Holy Spirit has called me and he has sent me to set these lessons before those*
who are mature in faith!   I am compelled to do so!!!

The relationship of the Holy Spirit
continued...

The Holy Spirit's actions indicate personality
continued...

The Holy Spirit reproves

John 16:7–11 7 Nevertheless I tell you the truth; It is expedient for you that I go away: for if I go not away, the Comforter will not come unto you; but if I depart, I will send him unto you. 8 And when he is come, he will reprove the world of sin, and of righteousness, and of judgment;

9 Of sin, because they believe not on me; 10 Of righteousness, because I go to my Father, and ye see me no more; 11 Of judgment, because the prince of this world is judged.

The acts which can be performed by the Holy Spirit indicate personality

He can be obeyed

Acts 10:19, 20 *My note: The Holy Spirit spoke to Peter and Peter obeyed the Holy Spirit.*

10:19 While Peter thought on this vision, the Spirit said unto him, Behold, three men seek thee.
10:20 Arise therefore, and get thee down, and go with them, doubting nothing: for I have sent them.

He can be lied to

Acts 5:3 But Peter said, Ananias, why hath Satan filled thine heart to lie to the Holy Ghost,
and to keep back *part* of the price of the land?
Acts 5:4 … ? thou hast not lied unto men, but unto God.

My note: *You cannot lie to an influence, but you can lie to a person.*

He can be resisted and tempted

Acts 7:51 Ye stiffnecked and uncircumcised in heart and ears, ye do always resist the Holy Ghost:
as your fathers *did*, so *do* ye.

Acts 5:9 Then Peter said unto her, How is it that ye have agreed together to tempt the Spirit of the Lord?

He can be grieved

Ephesians 4:30 And grieve not the holy Spirit of God, whereby ye are sealed unto the day of redemption.

The Holy Spirit reproves
continued…

John 16:7-11

Expedient, *n.* *That which serves to promote or advance; any means which may be employed to accomplish an end.*

Reprove, *v.t.*   *1. To* *blame* *; to censure.* *4. To* *convince* *of a* *fault, or to make it manifest.* **John xvi**
2. To charge with a *fault* *to the face; to chide; to reprehend.* **Luke iii**
6. To excite a sense of guilt.

> **Blame**, *v.t.* *1. To find* *fault* *with*
>
> > **Fault**, *n.* *[fail]* *1. Properly, an erring or missing; a failing*
>
> **Convince**, *v.t.*   *1. To persuade or satisfy the mind by evidence*
> *2. To convict; to prove guilty*
> *3. To evince ; to prove*

Re, *a prefix or inseparable participle in the composition of words, denotes* return, repetition, iteration.
> ***and***
Prove, *v.t.* *[…, to pierce, to penetrate, to send by force. The primary sense is to strain, to urge by force, or rather to thrust or drive. …]*

> *2. To* evince, *establish or ascertain as truth, reality or fact, by testimony or other evidence. The plaintif in a suit, must prove the truth of his declaration; the prosecutor must prove his charges against the accused.*

> ******Evince***, *v.t.* *[… , to vanquish, to prove or show; …, to conquer.]*
> *1. To show in a clear manner ; to prove beyond any reasonable doubt ; to manifest; to make evident.*

These three declare that Christ is God manifest in the flesh

John 16:9 Of sin,   *My note*: *Because, they believe not on Christ; their sin remains on them.*

John 16:10 Of righteousness,   *My note*: *Because, Christ ascending unto the Father affirms HIS righteousness; in which, Christ's righteousness convicts the world of sin and declares HIS righteousness.*

John 16:11 Of judgment,   *My note*: *Because, Christ ascending unto the Father proves that HE is who HE says HE is; which places judgment upon this world and the prince of this world, the Devil.*

Deity of
the Spirit of God / the Spirit / the Holy Ghost / the Holy Spirit

Genesis 1:1 In the beginning God created the heaven and the earth. **2** And the earth was without form, and void; and darkness *was* upon the face of the deep. And the Spirit of God moved upon the face of the waters. **3** And God said, Let there be light: and there was light.

Romans 8:9 But ye are not in the flesh, but in the Spirit, if so be that the Spirit of God dwell in you. Now if any man have not the Spirit of Christ, he is none of his. **10** And if Christ *be* in you, the body *is* dead because of sin; but the Spirit *is* life because of righteousness. **11** But if the Spirit of him that raised up Jesus from the dead dwell in you, he that raised up Christ from the dead shall also quicken your mortal bodies by his Spirit that dwelleth in you.

1John 5:7 For there are three that bear record in heaven, the Father, the Word, and the Holy Ghost: and these three are one.

Luke 11:13 If ye then, being evil, know how to give good gifts unto your children: how much more shall *your* heavenly Father give the Holy Spirit to them that ask him?

His names indicate deity

Romans 8:14 For as many as are led by the Spirit of God, they are the sons of God.

John 14:16, 17 16 And I will pray the Father, and he shall give you another Comforter, that he may abide with you for ever; 17 *Even* the Spirit of truth; whom the world cannot receive, because it seeth him not, neither knoweth him: but ye know him; for he dwelleth with you, and shall be in you.

John 14:26 But the Comforter, *which is* the Holy Ghost, whom the Father will send in my name, he shall teach you all things, and bring all things to your remembrance, whatsoever I have said unto you.

John 15:26 But when the Comforter is come, whom I will send unto you from the Father, *even* the Spirit of truth, which proceedeth from the Father, he shall testify of me:

Acts 5:9 Then Peter said unto her, How is it that ye have agreed together to tempt the Spirit of the Lord ? behold,
Read: 5: 3, 4 the feet of them which have buried thy husband *are* at the door, and shall carry thee out.

Romans 8:2 For the law of the Spirit of life in Christ Jesus hath made me free from the law of sin and death.

Matthew 12:28 But if I cast out devils by the Spirit of God, then the kingdom of God is come unto you.

1Corinthians 3:16 Know ye not that ye are the temple of God, and *that* the Spirit of God dwelleth in you?

Matthew 10:20 For it is not ye that speak, but the Spirit of your Father which speaketh in you.

John 16:13 Howbeit when he, the Spirit of truth, is come, he will guide you into all truth: for he shall not speak of himself; but whatsoever he shall hear, *that* shall he speak: and he will shew you things to come.

Luke 4:18 The Spirit of the Lord *is* upon me, because he hath anointed me to preach the gospel to the poor; he hath sent me to heal the brokenhearted, to preach deliverance to the captives, and recovering of sight to the blind, to set at liberty them that are bruised,

2Corinthians 3:3 *Forasmuch as ye are* manifestly declared to be the epistle of Christ ministered by us, written not with ink, but with the Spirit of the living God; not in tables of stone, but in fleshly tables of the heart.

Ephesians 1:13 In whom ye also *trusted*, after that ye heard the word of truth, the gospel of your salvation: in whom also after that ye believed, ye were sealed with that holy Spirit of promise,

Philippians 1:19 For I know that this shall turn to my salvation through your prayer, and the supply of the Spirit of Jesus Christ,

Hebrews 9:14 How much more shall the blood of Christ, who through the eternal Spirit offered himself without spot to God, purge your conscience from dead works to serve the living God?

Hebrews 10:29 Of how much sorer punishment, suppose ye, shall he be thought worthy, who hath trodden under foot the Son of God, and hath counted the blood of the covenant, wherewith he was sanctified, an unholy thing, and hath done despite unto the Spirit of grace ?

1Peter 1:11 Searching what, or what manner of time the Spirit of Christ which was in them did signify, when it testified beforehand the sufferings of Christ, and the glory that should follow. **12** Unto whom it was revealed, that not unto themselves, but unto us they did minister the things, which are now reported unto you by them that have preached the gospel unto you with the Holy Ghost sent down from heaven; which things the angels desire to look into.

Deity, *n.* 1. *Godhead ; divinity ; the nature and essence of the Supreme Being;*

> *as, the deity of the Supreme Being is manifest in his works.*

2. *God ; the Supreme Being, or infinite self-existing Spirit.*

1John 5:6,7,8   6 This is he that came by water and blood, *even* Jesus Christ; not by water only,
but by water and blood. And it is the Spirit that beareth witness, because the Spirit is truth.
7 For there are three that bear record in heaven, the Father, the Word, and the Holy Ghost:
and these three are one.
8 And there are three that bear witness in earth, the spirit, and the water, and the blood:
and these three agree in one.

> *My note*: *This verse declares Jesus Christ as bearing witness in earth, in the flesh as a man.*
> *Jesus Christ was God manifest in the flesh.*

1Timothy 3:16 And without controversy great is the mystery of godliness: God was manifest in the flesh, justified in
the Spirit, seen of angels, preached unto the Gentiles, believed on in the world, received up into glory.

Spirit, *n.* [*..., to breathe, to blow. The primary sense is <u>to rush or drive</u>.]*
1. *Primarily, wind; air in motion; hence, breath.*
2. *Animal excitement, or the effect of it; life; ardor; fire; courage; elevation of vehemence of mind.*
> *The troops attacked the enemy with great spirit.*

11. *Eagar desire; disposition of mind excited and directed to a particular object.*
21. *<u>The influence of the Holy Spirit</u>.*   **Matt. xxii**
Holy Spirit, the third person in the Trinity.

Matthew 22:43   41 While the Pharisees were gathered together, Jesus asked them, 42 Saying, **What think ye of
Christ? whose son is he?** They say unto him, *The son* of David. 43 He saith unto them,
How then doth David <u>in spirit</u> call him Lord, saying, 44 **The LORD said unto my
Lord, Sit thou on my right hand, till I make thine enemies thy footstool?** 45 **If David
then called him Lord, how is he his son?** 46 And no man was able to answer him a
word, neither durst any *man* from that day forth ask him any more *questions*.

My note: *The spirit is the action of a person; the soul is the emotion of a person and the body is the physical presence of a person.*
My note: *God's Spirit is HIS action.*   *Read:* James 2:26
My note: *"* <u>in spirit</u> *" is <u>a pressing forward</u> in knowing and in the knowledge of and in the power of the Holy Spirit.*

Isaiah 11:2 And <u>the spirit of the LORD</u> shall rest upon him, <u>the spirit of wisdom and understanding</u>,
<u>the spirit of counsel and might</u>, <u>the spirit of knowledge</u> and <u>of the fear of the LORD</u>;

Mark 1:10 And straightway coming up out of the water, he saw the heavens opened,
and <u>the Spirit</u> like a dove <u>descending upon him</u>:

Mark 1:12 And immediately <u>the spirit</u> <u>driveth him</u> into the wilderness.

Mark 2:8 And immediately when <u>Jesus perceived</u> <u>in his spirit</u> that they so reasoned within themselves,
he said unto them, **Why reason ye these things in your hearts?**

Luke 2:40 And <u>the child</u> grew, and waxed <u>strong in spirit</u>, <u>filled with wisdom</u>: and the grace of God was upon him.
My note: *"* the child *" is Jesus.*

Luke 3:22 And <u>the Holy Ghost descended</u> in a bodily shape like a dove upon him, and a voice came from heaven,
which said, Thou art my beloved Son; in thee I am well pleased.

Luke 4:1 And <u>Jesus being full of the Holy Ghost</u> returned from Jordan, and <u>was led by the Spirit</u> into the wilderness,

Luke 4:18   **The Spirit of the Lord** *is* **upon me, because <u>he hath anointed</u> me to preach the gospel to the poor;
<u>he hath sent me</u> to heal the brokenhearted, to preach deliverance to the captives, and
recovering of sight to the blind, to set at liberty them that are bruised,**

Read:
Matthew 26:40,41 ; **Mark** 14:38 ; **Luke** 1:17, 46,47 ; **John** 4:23,24 ; 6:63 ; 11:33 ; 13:21 ; **Acts** 6:10 ; 18:25 ; 19:21 ;
Romans 1:4,9 ; 2:29 ; **1Corinthians** 14:14,15; **2Corinthians** 4:13; **Colossians** 2:5,6; **1Timothy** 3:16 – 4:16; **2Timothy** 1:7–14

The attributes of the Holy Spirit are of Deity
distinctive features or characteristics

Attribute, n. That which is attributed; *that which is considered as belonging to, or inherent in;*
as, power and wisdom are attributes of the Supreme Being;

He is Omniscient
all knowing

1Corinthians 2:11,12   11 For what man knoweth the things of a man, save the spirit of man which is in him? even so the things of God knoweth no man, but the Spirit of God. 12 Now we have received, not the spirit of the world, but the spirit which is of God; that we might know the things that are freely given to us of God.

My note: God knows all and "the Spirit of God." is all knowing so, "the spirit which is of God;" is the desire and the focus and the knowledge of "all things that are freely given to us of God." ; seeking HIM out and desiring to do HIS will.

He is Omnipresent
everywhere present

Psalm 139:7-13   7 Whither shall I go from thy spirit? or whither shall I flee from thy presence? 8 If I ascend up into heaven, thou *art* there: if I make my bed in hell, behold, thou *art there.* 9 *If* I take the wings of the morning, *and* dwell in the uttermost parts of the sea; 10 Even there shall thy hand lead me, and thy right hand shall hold me. 11 If I say, Surely the darkness shall cover me; even the night shall be light about me. 12 Yea, the darkness hideth not from thee; but the night shineth as the day: the darkness and the light *are* both alike *to thee.* 13 For thou hast possessed my reigns: thou hast covered me in my mother's womb.

He is Omnipotent
all powerful

Genesis 1:1,2,3   1 In the beginning God created the heaven and the earth. 2 And the earth was without form, and void; and darkness *was* upon the face of the deep. And the Spirit of God moved upon the face of the waters. 3 And God said, Let there be light: and there was light.

Revelation 19:6   And I heard as it were the voice of a great multitude, and as the voice of many waters, and as the voice of mighty thunderings, saying, Alleluia: for the Lord God omnipotent reigneth.

Job 33:4   The spirit of God hath made me, and the breath of the Almighty hath given me life.

He is truth

1John 5:6   This is he that came by water and blood, *even* Jesus Christ; not by water only, but by water and blood. And it is the Spirit that beareth witness, because the Spirit is truth.

John 14:6   5 Thomas saith unto him, Lord, we know not whither thou goest; and how can we know the way?
6 Jesus saith unto him, I am the way, the truth, and the life: no man cometh unto the Father, but by me.

He is eternal

Hebrews 9:14   How much more shall the blood of Christ, who through the eternal Spirit offered himself without spot to God, purge your conscience from dead works to serve the living God?

He is called God

Acts 5:3,4   3 But Peter said, Ananias, why hath Satan filled thine heart to lie to the Holy Ghost, and to keep back *part* of the price of the land? 4 Whiles it remained, was it not thine own? and after it was sold, was it not in thine own power? why hast thou conceived this thing in thine heart? thou hast not lied unto men, but unto God.

The attributes of the Holy Spirit are of Deity

continued…

He is **Omniscient**

Omniscient, *a. Having universal knowledge or knowledge of all things; infinitely knowing; all-seeing;*
as the omniscient God,

Romans 8:27 And he that searcheth the hearts knoweth what *is* the mind of the Spirit, because he maketh intercession
Read: 8:1 - 39   for the saints according to *the will of* God.

He is **Omnipresent**

Omnipresent, *a. Present in all places at the same time; as the omnipresent Jehovah.*

My note: The Holy Spirit is (of) God. A person either has the Holy Spirit dwelling within him or he doesn't. The Holy Spirit does not come and go within a person. HE is in every one who is born again ; HE is in every believer ;
HE is in every child of God.

Psalm 139:13   *Possessed, pp. Held by lawful title; occupied; enjoyed; affected by demons or invisible agents.*

Reins, n. 1. The strap of a bridle, fastened to the curb or snaffle on each side, by which the rider of a horse
restrains and governs him.

Covered, pp. Spread over; hid; concealed; clothed; vailed; having a hat on; wrapped; inclosed;
sheltered; protected;

He is **Omnipotent**

Omnipotent, *a. Almighty; possessing unlimited power; all powerful.   The being that can create worlds must be omnipotent.*

Job 33:4   *My note: The Spirit of God   is   the breath of the Almighty.*   **Genesis 1:1,2,3** … **3** And God said, …

Genesis 2:7 And the LORD God formed man *of* the dust of the ground, and breathed into his nostrils the breath of life;
and man became a living soul.

He is **truth**

Read: **John 14:17** ; **15:26** ; **17:1 - 26**

John 14:6   *Way, n. 1. Literally, a passing; hence, a passage;*

Truth, n. 1. Conformity to fact or reality; exact accordance with that which is, or has been, or shall be.

Life, n. 24. The author and giver of supreme felicity.   **I am the way, the truth, and the life.** **John xiv** .

Felicity, n. [..., happy.] 1. Happiness, or rather great happiness ; … ; appropriately, the joys of heaven.

1John 5:6   *My note: blood is the lineage of the father*

Luke 1:35   **31** And, behold, thou shalt conceive in thy womb, and bring forth a son, and shalt call his name JESUS.

35 And the angel answered and said unto her, The Holy Ghost shall come upon thee, and the power of
the Highest shall overshadow thee: therefore also that holy thing which shall be born of thee shall
be called the Son of God.

John 1:1 **1** In the beginning was the Word, and the Word was with God, and the Word was God. **2** The same was in the
beginning with God. **3** All things were made by him; and without him was not any thing made that was made.
4 In him was life; and the life was the light of men. **5** And the light shineth in darkness; and the darkness
comprehended it not.

John 1:10   He was in the world, and the world was made by him, and the world knew him not.

John 1:14   And the Word was made flesh, and dwelt among us, (and we beheld his glory, the glory as of the only begotten
of the Father,) full of grace and truth.

John 1:29   The next day John seeth Jesus coming unto him, and saith, Behold the Lamb of God, which taketh away the sin
of the world.

Acts 20:28 Take heed therefore unto yourselves, and to all the flock, over the which the Holy Ghost hath made you
overseers, to feed the church of God, which he hath purchased   with his own blood.

His acts in relation to writing the word of God, show Deity

His work in revelation
the giving to man by the Spirit, what he could not otherwise know

Ephesians 3:3-6 3 How that by revelation he made known unto me the mystery; (as I wrote afore in few words, 4 Whereby, when ye read, ye may understand my knowledge in the mystery of Christ) 5 Which in other ages was not made known unto the sons of men, as it is now revealed unto his holy apostles and prophets by the Spirit; 6 That the Gentiles should be fellowheirs, and of the same body, and partakers of his promise in Christ by the gospel:

His work in inspiration

2Peter 1:21 For the prophecy came not in old time by the will of man: but holy men of God spake
as they were moved by the Holy Ghost.

2Timothy 3:16 All scripture *is* given by inspiration of God, and *is* profitable for doctrine, for reproof, for correction,
for instruction in righteousness:

His work in preserving His written word

1Corinthians 2:10 But God hath revealed *them* unto us by his Spirit: for the Spirit searcheth all things, yea, the deep things of God. 11 For what man knoweth the things of a man, save the spirit of man which is in him? even so the things of God knoweth no man, but the Spirit of God. 12 Now we have received, not the spirit of the world, but the spirit which is of God; that we might know the things that are freely given to us of God. 13 Which things also we speak, not in the words which man's wisdom teacheth, but which the Holy Ghost teacheth; comparing spiritual things with spiritual.

1Corinthians 2:9
But it is written, Eye hath not seen, nor ear heard, neither have entered into the heart of man, the things which God hath prepared for them that love him.

Isaiah 64:4
For since the beginning of the world *men* have not heard, nor perceived by the ear, neither hath the eye seen, O God, beside thee, *what* he hath prepared for him that waiteth for him.

Romans 3:10
10 As it is written, There is none righteous, no, not one: 11 There is none that understandeth, there is none that seeketh after God. 12 They are all gone out of the way, they are together become unprofitable; there is none that doeth good, no, not one. 13 Their throat *is* an open sepulchre; with their tongues they have used deceit; the poison of asps *is* under their lips: 14 Whose mouth *is* full of cursing and bitterness:

Psalm 5:9
For *there is* no faithfulness in their mouth; their inward part *is* very wickedness; their throat *is* an open sepulchre; they flatter with their tongue.

Psalm 10:7
His mouth is full of cursing and deceit and fraud: under his tongue *is* mischief and vanity.

Psalm 14:3
1 The fool hath said in his heart, *There is* no God. They are corrupt, they have done abominable works, *there is* none that doeth good. 2 The LORD looked down from heaven upon the children of men, to see if there were any that did understand, *and* seek God. 3 They are all gone aside, they are *all* together become filthy: *there is* none that doeth good, no, not one.

His work in giving understanding to the word of God

1Corinthians 2:14 But the natural man receiveth not the things of the Spirit of God: for they are foolishness unto him: neither can he know *them*, because they are spiritually discerned. 15 But he that is spiritual judgeth all things, yet he himself is judged of no man. 16 For who hath known the mind of the Lord, that he may instruct him?
But we have the mind of Christ.

His work in revelation

the giving to man, by the Spirit, what he could not otherwise know
continued...

<u>Galatians 1:12</u>   11 But I certify you, brethren, that the gospel which was preached of me is not after man.
12 For I neither received it of man, neither was I taught *it*, but by the <u>revelation</u> of Jesus Christ.

<u>Romans 16:25</u>   25 Now to him that is of power to stablish you according to my gospel, and the preaching of
Jesus Christ, according to <u>the revelation</u> of the mystery, which was kept secret since
the world began,   26 But now is made manifest, and by the scriptures of the prophets,
according to the commandment of the everlasting God, made known to all nations for
the obedience of faith: 27 To God only wise, *be* glory through Jesus Christ for ever.   A-men'.

His work in preserving His written word

continued...

<u>**My note:**</u> *The Lord Jesus Christ quoted many, many Scriptures, declaring them as absolute truth! The word of the LORD was*
inspired of the Holy Spirit and was written by inspired men of God.

<u>Scripture quoted by Jesus</u>: **Matthew 4:4,7,10; 11:10; 21:13; 26:24 ; ...**

<u>**Psalm 118:22**</u>   *was quoted many times by Jesus:*

The stone *which* the builders refused is become the head *stone* of the corner.

<u>**Matthew 21:42**</u>; <u>**Mark 12:10**</u> ; <u>**Luke 20:17**</u>; <u>**Acts 4:11**</u> ; <u>**Ephesians 2:20**</u> ; <u>**1Peter 2:6,7**</u>

<u>My note</u>: These are the words of Jesus.
<u>**Luke 20:17**</u> And he beheld them, and said, What is this then that is written,
The stone which the builders rejected, the same is become the head of the corner?

<u>**Isaiah 28:16**</u>
Therefore thus saith the Lord GOD, Behold, I lay in Zion for a foundation a stone, a tried stone,
a precious corner *stone*, a sure foundation: he that believeth shall not make haste.

<u>Acts 4:10 - 12</u>   10 Be it known unto you all, and to all the people of Israel, that by the name of <u>Jesus Christ of</u>
<u>Nazareth</u>, whom ye <u>crucified</u>, <u>whom God raised from the dead</u>, *even* by him doth this man stand
here before you whole. 11 <u>This is the stone which was set at nought of you builders, which is</u>
<u>become the head of the corner.</u> 12 Neither is there salvation in any other: for there is none other
name under heaven given among men, whereby we must be saved.

<u>My note</u>: These are the words of Jesus.
<u>**Luke 20:18**</u> Whosoever shall fall upon that stone shall be broken;
but on whomsoever it shall fall, it will grind him to powder.

<u>**Isaiah 8:13,14,15**</u>
13 Sanctify the LORD of hosts himself; and *let* him *be* your fear, and *let* him *be* your dread. 14 And he shall be for a sanctuary;
<u>but for a stone of stumbling and for a rock of offence to both the houses of Israel,</u> for a gin and for a snare to the inhabitants of
Jerusalem. 15 <u>And many among them shall stumble, and fall, and be broken</u>, and be snared, and be taken.

<u>**My note:**</u> *Also see:* <u>**Additional Scriptural References**</u> *to* <u>**His work in preserving His written word**</u>   <u>**pages 96 - 105**</u>

His work in giving understanding to the word of God

continued...

<u>*Judgeth,*</u> *v.t.*
<u>**Judge,**</u> *v.t.* **3.** <u>*Rightly to understand and discern.*</u>   He that is spiritual judgeth all things. <u>**1Cor. ii**</u> .

<u>*Judged,*</u> *pp. Heard and determined; tried judicially;* <u>*sentenced;*</u> *censured;* <u>*doomed.*</u>

<u>*Doom,*</u> *v.t.* **3.** *To pronounce sentence or judgment on.*
4. *To command authoritatively.*

<u>*Sentence,*</u> *n.* **1.** *In law, a judgment pronounced by a court or judge upon a criminal;*
<u>*Sentence,*</u> *v.t. To pass or pronounce the judgment of a court on; to doom;*
2. *To condemn; to doom to punishment.*

His acts in relation to salvation proves his deity

He reproves

John 16:8 And when he is come, he will reprove the world of sin, and of righteousness, and of judgment:

He regenerates

Titus 3:5 Not by works of righteousness which we have done, but according to his mercy he saved us, by the washing of regeneration, and renewing of the Holy Ghost;

John 3:3 Jesus answered and said unto him, Verily, verily, I say unto thee, Except a man be born again, he cannot see the kingdom of God.

Galatians 6:15 For in Christ Jesus neither circumcision availeth any thing, nor uncircumcision, but a new creature.

Titus 2:11 For the grace of God that bringeth salvation hath appeared to all men,

Colossians 2:10 And ye are complete in him, which is the head of all principality and power:

1Corinthians 12:13 For by one Spirit are we all baptized into one body, whether *we be* Jews or Gentiles, whether *we be* bond or free; and have been all made to drink into one Spirit.

Romans 6:3, 4 3 Know ye not, that so many of us as were baptized into Jesus Christ were baptized into his death? 4 Therefore we are buried with him by baptism into death: that like as Christ was raised up from the dead by the glory of the Father, even so we also should walk in newness of life.

Galatians 4:6,7 6 And because ye are sons, God hath sent forth the Spirit of his Son into your hearts, crying, Abba, Father. 7 Wherefore thou art no more a servant, but a son; and if a son, then an heir of God through Christ.

Colossians 3:10 And have put on the new *man*, which is renewed in knowledge after the image of him that created him:

Renewed, pp. Made new again;

Galatians 3:26 For ye are the children of God by faith in Christ Jesus.

Galatians 3:27 For as many of you as have been baptized into Christ have put on Christ.

He reproves
continued...

Reprove, *v.t.* *4. To convince of a fault, or to make it manifest.* **John xvi**

He regenerates

Titus 3:5
continued...

Regeneration, *n. 2. In theology, new birth by the grace of God; that change by which the will and natural enmity of man to God and his law are subdued, and a principle of supreme love to God and his law, or holy affections, are implanted in the heart.*

He saved us by the washing of regeneration and renewing of the Holy Spirit. **Tit. iii** .

Renew, *v.t.* *1. to restore to a former state, or to a good state, after decay or depravation.*
8. In theology, to make new; to renovate; to transform; to change from natural enmity to the love of God and his law; to implant holy affection in the heart; to regenerate. Be ye transformed by the renewing of your mind. **Rom. xii** . **Eph. iv**

Renewing, *ppr. Making new again ; re-establishing*

My note: Regeneration - the new birth
" by the washing of regeneration, " - *The new birth washes us; makes us clean*
"and the renewing of the Holy Ghost;"– *The Holy Ghost renews us; restores to us, intimacy with God*

2Corinthians 5:17 Therefore if any man *be* in Christ, *he is* a new creature: old things are passed away; behold, all things are become new.

1Corinthians 12:13 Drink – indicates to be absorbed or to be received
Into – noting the passing of a thing from one form or state to another

My note: Which signifies a definite change.

Romans 6:3,4 "baptized into Jesus Christ" *My note: Not water baptism*

Romans 6:23 For the wages of sin *is* death; but the gift of God *is* eternal life through Jesus Christ our Lord.

Galatians 4:6,7 6 And because ye are sons, God hath sent forth the Spirit of his Son into your hearts, crying, Abba, Father.
7 Wherefore thou art no more a servant, but a son; and if a son, then an heir of God through Christ.

Galatians 3:27 26 For ye are all the children of God by faith in Christ Jesus.
27 For as many of you as have been baptized into Christ have put on Christ.

My note: You are within Christ, and clothed by HIM, and HE is your cover and your shelter; because of being in Christ and being covered by HIM, we are able to rest in HIM and have a complete peace that we are HIS, now! and for ever!

My note: To put on Christ is to be in HIM ; we are HIS and we rest in HIM ; "unto the day of redemption." **Ephesians 4:30**
My note: "unto"- continually affirming
My note: "unto"- moving towards

Into - *noting the passing of a thing from one form or state to another*
Put on - *To invest with, as clothes or covering*
Invest, v.t. [..., to clothe. see Vest.]

The idea of " put on " is to rest in

Rest in confidence in Christ and not in the law
Trust in Christ and not in the law
He dwells within a believer, giving us HIS peace

John 14:26 But the Comforter, *which is* the Holy Ghost, whom the Father will send in my name, he shall teach you all things, and bring all things to your remembrance, whatsoever I have said unto you.

John 14:27 Peace I leave with you, my peace I give unto you: not as the world giveth, give I unto you. Let not your heart be troubled, neither let it be afraid.

Philippians 4:7 And the peace of God, which passeth all understanding, shall keep your hearts and minds through Christ Jesus.

He dwells within a believer

2Corinthians 4:3 – 7   3 But if our gospel be hid, it is hid to them that are lost: 4 In whom the god of this world hath blinded the minds of them which believe not, lest the light of the glorious gospel of Christ, who is the image of God, should shine unto them. 5 For we preach not ourselves, but Christ Jesus the Lord; and ourselves your servants for Jesus' sake. 6 For God, who commanded the light to shine out of darkness, hath shined in our hearts, to *give* the light of the knowledge of the glory of God in the face of Jesus Christ. 7 But we have this treasure in earthen vessels, that the excellency of the power may be of God, and not of us.

1Corinthians 3:16 Know ye not that ye are the temple of God, and *that* the Sprit of God dwelleth in you?

1Corinthians 6:19, 20   19 What? Know ye not that your body is the temple of the Holy Ghost *which is* in you, which ye have of God, and ye are not your own? 20 For ye are bought with a price: therefore glorify God in your body, and in your spirit, which are God's.

2Timothy 1:14   7 For God hath not given us the spirit of fear; but of power, and of love, and of a sound mind. 8 Be not therefore ashamed of the testimony of our Lord, nor of me his prisoner: but be thou partaker of the afflictions of the gospel according to the power of God; 9 Who hath saved us, and called us with an holy calling, not according to our works, but according to his own purpose and grace, which was given us in Christ Jesus before the world began. 13 Hold fast the form of sound words, which thou hast heard of me, in faith and love which is in Christ Jesus. 14 That good thing which was committed unto thee keep by the Holy Ghost which dwelleth in us.

Romans 8:9   9 But ye are not in the flesh, but in the Spirit, if so be *that* the Spirit of God dwell in you. Now if any man have not the Spirit of Christ, he is none of his. 10 And if Christ *be* in you, the body *is* dead because of sin; but the Spirit *is* life because of righteousness.

Romans 8:11 But if the Spirit of him that raised up Jesus from the dead dwell in you, he that raised up Christ from the dead shall also quicken your mortal bodies by his Spirit that dwelleth in you.

1Corinthians 3:16 Know ye not that ye are the temple of God, and that the Spirit of God dwelleth in you?

1Corinthians 6:19 What? know ye not that your body is the temple of the Holy Ghost *which is* in you, which ye have of God, and ye are not your own?

Romans 8:23 And not only *they*, but ourselves also, which have the firstfruits of the Spirit, even we ourselves groan within ourselves, waiting for the adoption, *to wit*, the redemption of our body.

2Corinthians 4:7 " this treasure " *is the Holy Ghost ;*
" earthen vessels " *is* " the temple " *and the temple is the body*

1Corinthians 6:19 " your body " " is " " the temple " " of the Holy Ghost " " *which is* in you,"

2Corinthians 5:5 Now he that hath wrought us for the selfsame thing *is* God, who also hath given unto us the earnest of the Spirit. 6 Therefore *we are* always confident, knowing that, whilst we are at home in the body, we are absent from the Lord:

Earnest, n. 2. First fruits; that which is in advance, and gives promise of something to come. Early fruit may be an earnest of fruit to follow. The first success in arms may be an earnest of future success. The christian's peace of mind in this life is an earnest of future peace and happiness. Hence, earnest or earnest-money is a first payment or deposit giving promise or assurance of full payment. Hence the practice of giving an earnest to ratify a bargain. This sense of the word is primary, denoting that which goes before, or in advance. Thus, the earnest of the spirit is given to saints, as a pledge or assurance of their future enjoyment of God's presence and favor.

My note: "earnest" is a guarantee
My note: God's "earnest of the Sprit." is HIS promise to all believers; the Holy Spirit declaring that we are HIS now and shall be with HIM, for ever!
My note: A promise of God is HIS word, which is absolute truth and is guaranteed by HIM to come to pass.
My note: What a special gift HE has given to each of HIS children; to have a peace of knowing that we are HIS, now and for ever !

Ephesians 3:16 14 For this cause I bow my knees unto the Father of our Lord Jesus Christ, 15 Of whom the whole family in heaven and earth is named, 16 That he would grant you, according to the riches of his glory, to be strengthened with might by his Spirit in the inner man; 17 That Christ may dwell in your hearts by faith; that ye, being rooted and grounded in love, 18 May be able to comprehend with all saints what *is* the breadth, and length, and depth, and height; 19 And to know the love of Christ, which passeth knowledge, that ye might be filled with all the fulness of God.

1John 3:24 And he that keepeth his commandments dwelleth in him, and he in him. And hereby we know that he abideth in us, by the Spirit which he hath given us.

1John 4:13 7 Beloved, let us love one another: for love is of God; and every one that loveth is born of God, and knoweth God. 8 He that loveth not knoweth not God; for God is love. 9 In this was manifested the love of God toward us, because that God sent his only begotten Son into the world, that we might live through him. 10 Herein is love, not that we loved God, but that he loved us, and sent his Son *to be* the propitiation for our sins. 11 Beloved, if God so loved us, we ought also to love one another. 12 No man hath seen God at any time. If we love one another, God dwelleth in us, and his love is perfected in us. 13 Hereby know we that we dwell in him, and he in us, because he hath given us of his Spirit. 14 And we have seen and do testify that the Father sent the Son *to be* the Saviour of the world. 15 Whosoever shall confess that Jesus is the Son of God, God dwelleth in him, and he in God. 16 And we have known and believed the love that God hath to us. God is love; and he that dwelleth in love dwelleth in God, and God in him.

1Cointhians 5:1 – 5 1 It is reported commonly *that there is* fornication among you, and such fornication as is not so much as named among the Gentiles, that one should have his father's wife. 2 And ye are puffed up, and have not rather mourned, that he that hath done this deed might be taken away from among you. 3 For I verily, as absent in body, but present in spirit, have judged already, as though I were present, *concerning* him that hath so done this deed, 4 In the name of our Lord Jesus Christ, when ye are gathered together, and my spirit, with the power of our Lord Jesus Christ, 5 To deliver such an one unto Satan for the destruction of the flesh, that the spirit may be saved in the day of the Lord Jesus.

My note: This focus of the flesh being destroyed and the spirit being saved is for one who is saved, so that, this person does not continually influence those around him, with this specific fornication and this specific sin. The holy Spirit of God is the seal of the King, declaring that we are HIS, for ever; we are to rest in HIM, unto the day of redemption; the day when our body is redeemed and glorified!
Read: **Ephesians 4:30**

1Corinthians 13:12
For now we see through a glass, darkly; but then face to face: now I know in part;
but then shall I know even as also I am known.
Read: 1Corinthians 13:1 – 13

He seals

Ephesians 4:30 And grieve not the holy Spirit of God, whereby ye are sealed unto the day of redemption.

Grieve – *to offend; to displease, to provoke*
Sealed – *unalterable; definite; absolute*
Unto – *continually affirming*

My note:
" sealed " *is the seal of the King; the seal is the Holy Spirit dwelling within every believer; declaring that we are HIS, for ever.*

Romans 8:23 And not only *they*, but ourselves also, which have the firstfruits of the Spirit,
even we ourselves groan within ourselves, waiting for the adoption,
to wit, the redemption of our body.

My note*:* " the adoption " *is* " the redemption of our body "

Wit, *v.i. To* know*. This verb is used only in the* infinitive*, to wit, namely,* that is to say*.* **My note***:* that is to say *;* restating it

Infinitive, *a. In grammar, the infinitive mode expresses the action of the verb, without limitation of person or number;*
as, to love.

Know, *v.t. [... The radical sense of knowing is generally to take, receive, or hold.]*
1. To perceive with certainty; to understand clearly; to have a clear and certain perception of truth, fact,
or any thing that actually exists.

Romans 8:15 For ye have not received the spirit of bondage again to fear;
but ye have received the Spirit of adoption, whereby we cry, Abba, Father.
Colossians 1:14 In whom we have redemption through his blood, *even* the forgiveness of sins:
Ephesians 1:7 In whom we have redemption through his blood, the forgiveness of sins,
according to the riches of his grace;
Hebrews 9:22 And almost all things are by the law purged with blood;
and without shedding of blood is no remission. *Read:* **Chapters 9 – 11**

Redemption, *n.* *1. Repurchase of captured goods or prisoners; the act of procuring the deliverance of persons or things from*
the possession and power of captors by the payment of an equivalent; ransom; release;
2. Deliverance from bondage, ...
6. In theology, the purchase of God's favor by the death and sufferings of Christ; the ransom or deliverance
of sinners from the bondage of sin and the penalties of God's violated law by the atonement of Christ.
In whom we have redemption through his blood. **Eph. i. Col. i.** *Dryden, Nelson,*

My note: Our body is still bound! How do we know this to be true? Because our body sees corruption; it dies, deteriorates,
breaks down and becomes dust. One day all who are HIS shall receive a glorified body; one which is free from sin
and corruption! One day our glorified body will be in Heaven, in the presence of our Lord and Saviour Jesus Christ!!!

WHAT A GLORIOUS DAY THIS IS!!!

My note:
The Holy Spirit is the seal of the KING; The seal of our LORD and SAVIOUR JESUS CHRIST !!!

1Timothy 6:13 - 17 **15** ... , the King of kings, and Lord of lords;
Revelation 19:16 ... , KING OF KINGS, AND LORD OF LORDS.

Ephesians 1:13,14 **13** In whom ye also *trusted*, after that ye heard the word of truth, the gospel of your salvation:
in whom also after that ye believed, ye were sealed with that holy Spirit of promise,
14 Which is the earnest of our inheritance until the redemption of the purchased possession,
unto the praise of his glory.

Earnest, *n. First fruits ; that which is in advance, and gives promise of something to come.*

My note:
The Holy Spirit dwelling within a believer confirms / declares that we are HIS !

My note:
This sealing of the Holy Ghost puts a believer in a state of not being able to be altered; it is fixed by God.

My note:

sealed → *birthright* → *by the authority of God* → *in the name of (through)* **the Lord Jesus Christ** → *with the Holy Spirit*

sealed → *birthright* → *new birth* → *born again* → *by God the Father* → *through Jesus Christ* → *with that holy* **Spirit of promise**

Birthright, *n. Any right or privilege, to which a person is entitled by birth*

Ephesians 1:13,14
My note: " sealed with that holy Spirit of promise,"

My note: Gospel, n. defined on page 43

Gospel, *n. [... god ... and spell ... or word ... .]*   *My note: **God's word ; God's message ; God's joyful message!***
Salvation, *n. [to save] 1. The act of saving ; preservation from destruction, danger or great calamity.*
2. Appropriately in theology, the redemption of man from the bondage of sin and liability to eternal death,
and the conferring on him everlasting happiness.

Believed, *pp. credited ; assented to, as true*   *True, a. 1. conformable to fact;*
Sealed, *pp. confirmed*   *Fact, n. Any thing done, or that comes to pass; an act; a deed;*
Confirmed, *pp. established*   *an effect produced or achieved; an event.*

Established, *pp. set ; fixed firmly ; founded ; ordained ; exacted ; ratified ; confirmed .*

My note: **The sealing** *(unalterable, absolute, definite)* **with the Holy Ghost is the guarantee** of our **inheritance** *(being with God in heaven)* **until the redemption of the purchased possession / our body** *(with our glorified body - " : old things are passed away; behold, all things are become new."* **2Corinthians 5:17** *)* **unto** *(continually affirming)* **the praise of his glory.**

1Peter 2:2 As newborn babes, desire the sincere milk of the word, that ye may grow thereby:

My note:
If a baby doesn't desire milk, there is something wrong with that baby!

Romans 6:4 Therefore we are buried with him by baptism into death: that like as Christ was raised up from the dead by the glory of the Father, even so we also should walk in newness of life.
Galatians 6:15 For in Christ Jesus neither circumcision availeth any thing, nor uncircumcision, but a new creature.
2Corinthians 5:17 Therefore if any man *be* in Christ, *he is* a new creature: old things are passed away; behold, all things are become new.
Ephesians 4:24 And that ye put on the new man, which after God is created in righteousness and true holiness.
Colossians 3:10 And have put on the new *man*, which is renewed in knowledge after the image of him that created him:
1Peter 1:23 Being born again, not of corruptible seed, but of incorruptible, by the word of God, which liveth and abideth for ever.
1John 2:29 If ye know that he is righteous, ye know that every one that doeth righteousness is born of him.
1John 5:4 For whosoever is born of God overcometh the world: and this is the victory that overcometh the world, *even* our faith.

Children of God

Romans 8:16, 17 16 The Spirit itself beareth witness with our spirit, that we are the children of God: 17 And if children, then heirs; heirs of God, and joint-heirs with Christ; if so be that we suffer with *him*, that we may be also glorified together.
Romans 9:26 And it shall come to pass, *that* in the place where it was said unto them, Ye *are* not my people; there shall they be called the children of the living God.
Galatians 3:26 For ye are all the children of God by faith in Christ Jesus.
Ephesians 5:1 Be ye therefore followers of God, as dear children;
Ephesians 5:8 For ye were sometimes darkness, but now *are ye* light in the Lord: walk as children of light:
1Thessalonians 5:5 Ye are the children of light, and the children of the day: we are not of the night, nor of darkness.
1Peter 1:14 As obedient children, not fashioning yourselves according to the former lusts in your ignorance:

My note:
All of God's children are sealed in Jesus Christ; by the power of the Holy Spirit and all to the glory of God the Father!!!

UNALTERABLE!

Romans 8:17 ...; heirs of God, and joint-heirs with Christ; ...

He fills
to be under the control or influence of the Holy Spirit of God
My note:
The Holy Ghost dwells within every believer however, His presence is more evident as we yield unto Him.

Ephesians 5:17 – 20   17 Wherefore be ye not unwise, but understanding what the will of the Lord *is*.
18 And be not drunk with wine, wherein is excess; but be filled with the Spirit;
19 Speaking to yourselves in psalms and hymns and spiritual songs, singing and making melody in your heart to the Lord; 20 Giving thanks always for all things unto God and the Father in the name of our Lord Jesus Christ;

Unwise, *a.   not choosing the best means for the end;*

Understanding, *n. The faculty of the human mind by which it apprehends the real state of things presented to it, or by which it receives or comprehends the ideas which others express or intend to communicate.*
Luke xxiv . Eph. i .
There is a spirit in man, and the inspiration of the Almighty giveth him understanding. **Job xxxii** .

1John 5:21   20 And we know that the Son of God is come, and hath given us an understanding, that we may know him that is true, and we are in him that is true, *even in* his Son Jesus Christ. This is the true God, and eternal life. **21** Little children, keep yourselves from idols. A-men'.

Filled – *According to Scripture: Being filled with, is being controlled by or under the influence of and yielding unto that influence, such as, one who is not able to resist or does not desire to resist the influence of the Holy Ghost; communing with him in a less restrictive mindset and in a more embracing mindset; communing with Him in the spirit mind. The more we sincerely praise the Lord Jesus Christ and do His will, the greater our intimacy with the Holy Spirit is and becomes: true intimacy with Him is delightful and it is peaceful!*

Two things involved in being filled with the Holy Ghost

Yielding unto God
Unto – continually affirming
Romans 6:13   Neither yield ye your members *as* instruments of unrighteousness unto sin: but yield yourselves unto God, as those that are alive from the dead, and your members *as* instruments of righteousness unto God.

Presenting yourself unto God

Romans 12:1,2   1 I beseech you therefore, brethren, by the mercies of God, that ye present your bodies a living sacrifice, holy, acceptable unto God, *which is* your reasonable service.
2 And be not conformed to this world: but be ye transformed by the renewing of your mind, that ye may prove what *is* that good, and acceptable, and perfect, will of God.

Titus 3:5   Not by works of righteousness which we have done, but according to his mercy he saved us, by the washing of regeneration, and renewing of the Holy Ghost;

My note: "washing of regeneration" *is the* "renewing of the Holy Ghost;" *born again.*
Regeneration, *n. the act of producing anew.*

<u>Yielding unto God</u>

Romans 6:13

<u>Instrument</u>, *n.* **2.** *That which is* <u>subservient</u> *to the execution of any effect; means used or contributing to any effect;*
applicable to persons or things.

5. *A person which acts for another, or is employed by another for a special purpose, ...*

<u>Subservient</u>, *a. Useful as an instrument to promote a purpose; serving to promote some end.*

<u>Unrighteousness</u>, *n. Injustice;* <u>a violation of the divine law</u>, *or of the plain principles of justice and equity; wickedness.*

<u>Righteousness</u>, *n. Purity of heart and rectitude of life;* <u>conformity of heart and life to the divine law</u>. *Righteousness, as used in Scripture and theology, in which it is chiefly used, is nearly equivalent to holiness, comprehending holy principles and affections of heart, and conformity of life to the divine law. It includes all we call justice, honesty and virtue, with holy affections; in short,* <u>it is true religion</u>.

<u>My note</u>: *Conformity of heart and life to the divine law,* <u>true religion</u>, *can only be found in the Lord Jesus Christ; by the power of the Holy Spirit and all to the glory of God the Father.*

Matthew 22:36-40 36 Master, which *is* the great commandment in the law? **37** Jesus said unto him, Thou shalt love the Lord thy God with all thy heart, and with all thy soul, and with all thy mind. 38 This is the first and great commandment. 39 And the second *is* like unto it, Thou shalt love thy neighbour as thyself. 40 <u>On these two commandments hang all the law and the prophets.</u>

<u>Presenting yourself unto God</u>

Romans 12:1,2

<u>Beseech</u>, *v.t.* <u>to ask or pray with urgency</u>; *followed by a person; as,*   " I Paul beseech you by the meekness of Christ," **2Cor. x** .

<u>Mercies</u>,
<u>Mercy</u>, *n.* **1.** *That benevolence, mildness or tenderness of heart which disposes a person to overlook injuries, or to treat an offender better than he deserves; the disposition that tempers justice, and induces an injured person to forgive trespasses and injuries, and to forbear punishment, or inflict less than law or justice will warrant. ...*
Mercy is a distinguishing attribute of the Supreme Being.

The Lord is long-suffering and of great mercy, forgiving iniquity and transgression,
and by no means clearing the guilty. **Num. xiv** .

<u>Present</u>, *v.t.* [*..., before, and ..., to be.*] **1.** *To set, place or introduce into the presence or* <u>before the face of a superior</u>,
4. <u>To give</u>; <u>to offer</u> *gratuitously for reception.*

<u>Holy</u>, *a. Hallowed; consecrated or* <u>set apart to a sacred use</u>, *or to the service of worship of God; a sense frequent in Scripture;*

<u>Conformed</u>, *pp.* <u>Made to resemble</u>; <u>reduced to a likeness of</u>; <u>made agreeable to</u>; *suited.*

<u>Transformed</u>, *pp.* <u>Renewed</u> ;   <u>Renewed</u>, *pp Made new again* ;   <u>My note</u>: <u>Renew</u>, *v.t.* <u>defined on page 43</u>
<u>Transform</u>, *v.t.* **3.** *In theology, to change the natural disposition and temper of man from a state of enmity to God and his law, into the image of God, or into a disposition and temper conformed to the will of God.*

Be ye transformed by the renewing of your mind. **Rom. xii** .

<u>Prove</u>, *v.t.* **2.** *To evince, establish or ascertain as* <u>truth</u>, <u>reality</u> *or* <u>fact</u>, *by testimony or other evidence.*
5. *To experience; to try by suffering or encountering;* <u>to gain certain knowledge</u> *by the operation of something on ourselves, or by some act of our own.*

<u>My note</u>: <u>Prove</u> – *to be found certain or true* **Romans 12:2** ... , that ye may prove what *is* that good, and acceptable, and perfect, will of God.

Symbols of the Holy Spirit's actions

A dove

Matthew 3:16 And Jesus, when he was baptized, went up straightway out of the water: and, lo, the heavens were opened unto him, and he saw the Spirit of God descending like a dove, and lighting upon him:

Mark 1:10 And straightway coming up out of the water, he saw the heavens opened, and the Spirit like a dove descending upon him:

Luke 3:22 And the Holy Ghost descending in a bodily shape like a dove upon him, and a voice came from heaven, which said, Thou art my beloved Son; in thee I am well pleased.

John 1:32 And John bare record, saying, I saw the Spirit descending from heaven like a dove, and it abode upon him.

The earnest

2Corinthians 5:5 Now he that hath wrought us for the selfsame thing *is* God, who also hath given unto us the earnest of the Spirit.

Fire

Acts 2:3 And there appeared unto them cloven tongues like as of fire, and it sat upon each of them.

Oil

Luke 4:18 The Spirit of the Lord *is* upon me, because he hath anointed me to preach the gospel to the poor; he hath sent me to heal the brokenhearted, to preach deliverance to the captives, and recovering of sight to the blind, to set at liberty them that are bruised,

My note: Anointed is to consecrate or set apart for a sacred use; Jesus was/is the Lord's ANOINTED!!!

James 5:14 Is any sick among you? let him call for the elders of the church; and let them pray over him,

My note: anointing with oil – a comfort renewed.   anointing him with oil in the name of the Lord:

Acts 10:38 How God anointed Jesus of Nazareth with the Holy Ghost and with power: who went about doing good, and healing all that were oppressed of the devil; for God was with him.

My note: Jesus was set apart as THE SERVANT of GOD, for a sacred purpose.

2Corinthians 1:21 Now he which stablisheth us with you in Christ, and hath anointed us, *is* God;

My note: Anointed is to be set apart for a sacred use or purpose.

Sealed

My note: This seal of the Holy Ghost is the declaration of ownership / birthright and is fixed, permanently!!!

2Corinthians 1:22 Who hath also sealed us, and given the earnest of the Spirit in our hearts.

Ephesians 1:13 In whom ye also *trusted*, after that ye heard the word of truth, the gospel of your salvation: in whom also after that ye believed, ye were sealed with that holy Spirit of promise,

Ephesians 4:30 And grieve not the holy Spirit of God, whereby ye are sealed unto the day of redemption.

Water

John 4:14 But whosoever drinketh of the water that I shall give him shall never thirst; but the water that I shall give him shall be in him a well of water springing up into everlasting life.

John 7:38,39 38 He that believeth on me, as the scripture hath said, out of his belly shall flow rivers of living water. 39 (But this spake he of the Spirit, which they that believe on him should receive: for the Holy Ghost was not yet *given*; because that Jesus was not yet glorified.)

Wind

John 3:8 The wind bloweth where it listeth, and thou hearest the sound thereof, but canst not tell whence it cometh, and whither it goeth: so is every one that is born of the Spirit.

Acts 2:2 And suddenly there came a sound from heaven as of a rushing mighty wind,

My note: " it " is " a sound "   and it filled all the house where they were sitting.

A dove

Matthew 3:16 … the Spirit of God <u>descending</u> <u>like</u> a dove, and <u>lighting</u> upon him:

Like, *adv.* *1. In the same manner.*

Lighting   **Light**, *v.i.* **4.** *To settle; to rest;*

John 1:32   *My note: The Holy Ghost rested or remained upon Jesus.*

Abode, *pret. of abide.*
Abide, v.i. pret. and part. abode [*to be, or exist, to continue; … to dwell, rest, continue, stand firm, or be stationary for any time indefinitely.*]

      1. *To rest, or dwell.* <u>Gen. xxix19</u>   **4.** *To remain, to continue.* <u>Acts. xxvii 31</u> ; <u>Eccles. viii 15</u> .

My note: In each of the Gospels, dove is in reference to the action of the Holy Ghost descending upon Jesus and a description of the descending being, "like a dove". The Holy Spirit settled (descended) upon Jesus as a dove settles (descends) upon the earth.

Fire

Malachi 3:2,3   **2** But who may abide the day of his coming? and who shall stand when he appeareth? for he *is* like a refiner's fire, and like fullers' soap: **3** And he shall sit *as* a refiner and purifier of silver: and he shall purify the sons of Levi, and purge them as gold and silver, that they may offer unto the LORD an offering in righteousness.

These descriptions of 1-7 were set before me of the Holy Spirit

1. A **dove** *is a clean, gentle bird*   **Dove**, *n. A word of endearment, or an emblem of innocence.*
    My references: <u>Song of Solomon 2:14</u> ; <u>5:2;6:9;1:15;4:1</u>

    <u>Genesis 8:8-12</u> *My note: The dove returned with confirmation that the LORD's wrath had passed; giving peace to Noah, who was the servant of the LORD.*

2. **Earnest** *is the guarantee*   **Earnest**, *n. First fruits; that which is in advance, and gives promise of something to come.*

3. **Fire** *is a refiner; purging impurities.* *Fire – to rush; light; luster; spendor*   *My note: Fire declares the authority of the Lord!*
    Fire, n. *[… to rush …]* **4.** *light ; luster ;*   **Deuteronomy 4:24; 9:3** ; **Hebrews 12:29**

4. **Oil** *is a renewer. (* <u>anointed</u> *with oil – a* <u>comfort</u> *renewed)*   **Comfort**, *n. The word signifies properly new strength, or animation;*
    Comfort, *v.t.* [*… to relieve or help … and … strong.*]

  Anointed, *pp.* set apart   **Hebrews 1:9** Thou hast loved righteousness, and hated iniquity; therefore God, *even* thy God, hath <u>anointed thee with the oil of gladness</u> <u>above thy fellows</u>.
    Isaiah 61:3 … <u>oil of joy</u> …

See: **Additional Scriptural References:** *pages 109 – 113*   *My note:* **Consolation** *, n.   defined on page 111*

    Anoint, v.t. **4.** *To prepare, …   (* <u>Webster's note</u>*: To anoint the head with oil,* **Ps. xxiii**, *seems to signify to communicate the* <u>consolations</u> *of the Holy Spirit.*)

    Words of Jesus: <u>Luke 4:18</u> **"me"** *is Jesus* *and* **"he"** *is* **"The Spirit of the Lord"**

Luke 4:18,19 18 The Spirit of the Lord *is* <u>upon</u> **me**, because **he** <u>hath anointed</u> **me** to preach the gospel to the poor; **he** <u>hath sent</u> **me** to heal the brokenhearted, to preach deliverance to the captives, and recovering of sight to the blind, to set at liberty them that are bruised, 19 To preach the acceptable year of the Lord.

Luke 4:21 And he began to say unto them, This day is this scripture fulfilled in your ears.
    Isaiah fulfilled: **Isaiah 61:1,2**   *My note: Also,* <u>Mark 1:24</u> ; <u>Acts 2:27</u> ; <u>3:14,15</u> ; <u>13:35</u> ; <u>Psalm 89:18,20</u>

5. **Seal** *is of permanence.*   *My note: We are in Christ, (sealed) and we are of Christ (sealed) ;* <u>We are safe and secure!</u>

See: **Additional Scriptural References:** *page 115*   <u>We are His, now and for ever!!!</u>

    Seal, *v.t.* **2.** *To set or affix a seal, as a mark of authenticity;* **3.** *To confirm; to ratify; to establish.*
        8. *To mark as one's own property, and secure from danger.*
    Sealed, *pp. Furnished with a seal; fastened with a seal; confirmed; closed.*

6. **Water** *fills and satisfies.* **Psalm 107:9**

7. **Wind** *is a power unseen. (to move, flow, rush, drive along); The Holy Spirit comes and goes, like the wind ; unseen, but evident!*

My note: The coming and going, as the wind, is not referring to the Holy Ghost in and out of a believer; as if one is saved and then one is not saved. If one is born again, he is the Lord's now and for ever, and he has the Holy Spirit continually dwelling within him, declaring him to be a child of God !   **Ephesians 4:30** … <u>sealed unto the day of redemption.</u>

The Gifts of the Holy Spirit

A gift is something given or bestowed upon one, by God
such as:
The gift of salvation or an ability for serving God

Every believer has a gift or gifts for serving the Lord and these gifts are made manifest by the Holy Spirit

Read: 12:1 - 31

1Corinthians 12:1 Now concerning spiritual *gifts*, brethren, I would not have you ignorant.

1Corinthians 12:4 – 7   4 Now there are diversities of gifts, but the same Spirit. 5 And there are differences of administrations, but the same Lord. 6 And there are diversities of operations, but it is the same God which worketh all in all. 7 But the manifestation of the Spirit is given to every man to profit withal.

Manifestation, n. The act of disclosing what is secret, unseen or obscure; discovering to the eye or to the understanding; the exhibition of any thing by clear evidence; display; as the manifestation of God's power in creation, or of his benevolence in redemption.

1Corinthians 12:11 But all these worketh that one and the selfsame Spirit, dividing to every man severally as he will.
Severally, adv. Separately; distinctly; apart from others

Not all believers have the same gift or gifts

1Corinthians 12:23,30   29 *Are* all apostles? *are* all prophets? *are* all teachers? *are* all workers of miracles?   30 Have all the gifts of healing? do all speak with tongues? do all interpret?

What are we to do with our gift / ability?

We are to serve

My note: **First**, *I am to* love God *and* the Lord Jesus Christ my Saviour *and* praise HIM *for* HIS *gift of salvation and for* HIS *gift of the Holy Ghost, who declares that I am* HIS; *now and for ever.* **Second**, *I am to* serve HIM within my own family. **Third**, *I am to* serve HIM within the body of believers. **And**, *I am to* serve HIM in witnessing to those who are lost; *All by the leading of the Spirit of God and with the encouragement of fellow believers, especially those who are mature in the faith.*

First   *I am to,* love God *and* praise HIM .

Love the Lord thy God

Deuteronomy 6:4,5,6   4 Hear, O Israel: The LORD our God *is* one LORD: 5 And thou shalt love the LORD thy God with all thine heart, and with all thy soul, and with all thy might.   6 And these words, which I command thee this day, shall be in thine heart:

Deuteronomy 10:12 And now, Israel, what doth the LORD thy God require of thee, but to fear the LORD thy God, to walk in all his ways, and to love him, and to serve the LORD thy God with all thy heart and with all thy soul,

Deuteronomy 11:1 Therefore thou shalt love the LORD thy God, and keep his charge, and his statutes, and his judgments, and his commandments, alway.

Joshua 23:11 Take good heed therefore unto yourselves, that ye love the LORD your God.

Psalm 18:1 – 3   1 I will love thee, O LORD, my strength. 2 The LORD *is* my rock, and my fortress, and my deliverer; my God, my strength, in whom I will trust; my buckler, and the horn of my salvation, *and* my high tower.   3 I will call upon the LORD, *who is worthy* to be praised: so shall I be saved from mine enemies.

Psalm 97:10 Ye that love the LORD, hate evil: he preserveth the souls of his saints; he delivereth them out of the hand of the wicked.

Psalm 116:1 I love the LORD, because he hath heard my voice *and* my supplications.

Matthew 22:36-40 36 Master, which *is* the great commandment in the law? 37 Jesus said unto him, **Thou shalt love the Lord thy God with all thy heart, and with all thy soul, and with all thy mind.** 38 **This is the first and great commandment.** 39 **And the second** is **like unto it, Thou shalt love thy neighbour as thyself.**   40 **On these two commandments hang all the law and the prophets.**

Praise HIS name
Praise, v.t. [... ; *to praise, extol or lift up*; *to prize, to value*; *to boast or glory*. ...] *2. to magnify* **Ps. cxlviii**

Psalm 9:1,2   1 I will praise *thee*, O LORD, with my whole heart; I will shew forth all thy marvellous works.   2 I will be glad and rejoice in thee: I will sing praise to thy name, O thou most High.

Psalm 18:1–3 ; 66:1,2 ; 92:1 ; 95:1-3 ; 105: 1-3 ; 106:1 ; 108:1–5 ; 111:1 ; 112:1 ; 113:1 ; 117:1,2 ; 135:1–3 ; 138:1 ; 146:1,2 ; 147:1 ;
Luke 18:43 *and* **Luke 19:9 – 41**   148:1–5 ; 150:1–6

Philippians 1:11 Being filled with the fruits of righteousness, which are by Jesus Christ, unto the glory and praise of God.

Revelation 19:1 – 9 5 And a voice came out of the throne, saying, Praise our God, all ye his servants, and ye that fear him, both small and great.

The Gifts of the Holy Spirit
We are to serve
continued...

Second *I am to, serve HIM within my own family .*

1Timothy 5:8 But if any provide not for his own, and specially for those of his own house,
Infidel, n. defined on page 43   he hath denied the faith, and is worse than an infidel.

Ephesians 5:1,2 1 Be ye therefore followers of God, as dear children; 2 And walk in love, as Christ also hath loved
Read: 4:32 – 6:24   us, and hath given himself for us an offering and a sacrifice to God for a sweetsmelling savour.

Ephesians 5:22 Wives, submit yourselves unto your own husbands, as unto the Lord.

Ephesians 5:25 Husbands, love your wives, even as Christ also loved the church, and gave himself for it;

Ephesians 5:28 So ought men to love their wives as their own bodies. He that loveth his wife loveth himself.

Ephesians 6:1 Children, obey your parents in the Lord: for this is right.

Ephesians 6:4 And, ye fathers, provoke not your children to wrath: but bring them up in the nurture and
admonition of the Lord.

Nurture, n. [... , to nourish.] 1. That which nourishes; 2. That which promotes growth ; education ; instruction. **Eph. vi** .
Nourish, v.t. 3. To supply the means of support and increase; to encourage ; 4. To cherish; to comfort ; **James v.**

Admonition, n. Gentle reproof; counseling against a fault; instructions in duties; caution; direction. **Tit. iii** . **1Cor. x**

Third *I am to, serve HIM within the body of believers .*

Matthew 22:37-40 37 Jesus said unto him, **Thou shalt love the Lord thy God with all thy heart, and with all thy soul, and with all thy mind.** 38 **This is the first and great commandment.** 39 **And the second *is* like unto it, Thou shalt love thy neighbour as thyself.** 40 **On these two commandments hang all the law and the prophets.**

Mark 12:29,30,31 29 And Jesus answered him, **The first of all the commandments *is*, Hear, O Israel; The Lord our God is one Lord:** 30 **And thou shalt love the Lord thy God with all thy heart, and with all thy soul, and with all thy mind, and with all thy strength: this *is* the first commandment.** 31 **And the second *is* like, *namely* this, Thou shalt love thy neighbour as thyself. There is none other commandment greater than these.**

John 13:34, 35 34 **A new commandment I give unto you, That ye love one another; as I have loved you, that ye also love one anther.** 35 **By this shall all *men* know that ye are my disciples, if ye have love one to another.**

1John 3:23,24 23 And this is his commandment, That we should believe on the name of his Son Jesus Christ, and love one another, as he gave us commandment. 24 And he that keepeth his commandments dwelleth in him, and he in him. And hereby we know that he abideth in us, by the Spirit which he hath given us.

My note: The Holy Ghost dwelling in us enlightens a child of God to the truth (fact, knowledge, knowing) that the fullness of God (the Father, the Son, and the Holy Ghost) dwells in us and we dwell in HIM , the fullness of God . Read: **John 14:1 – 15:27**

John 15:12,13 8 **Herein is my Father glorified, that ye bear much fruit; so shall ye be my disciples.** 9 **As the Father hath loved me, so have I loved you: continue ye in my love.** 10 **If ye keep my commandments, ye shall abide in my love; even as I have kept my Father's commandments, and abide in his love.** 11 **These things have I spoken unto you, that my joy might remain in you, and *that* your joy might be full.** 12 **This is my commandment, That ye love one another, as I have loved you,** 13 **Greater love hath no man than this, that a man lay down his life for his friends.**

And ...

I am to, serve HIM in witnessing to those around me; to whosoever the Holy Spirit declares .

Matthew 28:18-20 18 And Jesus came and spake unto them, saying, **All power is given unto me in heaven and in earth.** 19 **Go ye therefore, and teach all nations, baptizing them in the name of the Father, and of the Son, and of the Holy Ghost:** 20 **Teaching them to observe all things whatsoever I have commanded you: and, lo, I am with you alway, *even* unto the end of the world.** A-men'.

Christic came to serve

We are to serve one another in the love of Jesus, our LORD and SAVIOUR

HE always did the will of HIS FATHER!!!

Hebrews 9:14 How much more shall the blood of <u>Christ</u>, who <u>through the eternal Spirit</u> <u>offered himself</u> <u>without spot to God</u>, purge your conscience from dead works to serve the living God ?

Matthew 20:28 Even <u>the Son of man came</u> not to be ministered unto, but <u>to minister</u>, and <u>to give his life a ransom for many</u>.

Mark 10:44,45 44 And whosoever of you will be chiefest, shall be servant of all. 45 For even <u>the Son of man came</u> not to be ministered unto, but <u>to minister, and</u> <u>to give his life a ransom for many</u>.

Hebrews 8:1 Now of the things which we have spoken *this is* the sum: <u>We have such an high priest,</u> <u>who is set on the right hand of the throne of the Majesty in the heavens;</u>

Hebrews 8:6,7,8 6 But now hath he obtained a more excellent ministry, by how much also <u>he is the mediator of a better</u> <u>covenant</u>, which was established upon better promises. 7 For if that <u>first *covenant*</u> had been faultless, then should no place have been sought for the second. 8 For <u>finding fault with them</u>, he saith, Behold, the days come, saith the Lord, when I will make a <u>new covenant</u> with the house of Israel and with the house of Judah:

> <u>Covenant</u>, *n. [... Literally, a coming together; a meeting or agreement of minds.]* **3.** *In theology, ... <u>The covenant of redemption,</u>* <u>*is the mutual agreement between the Father and Son, respecting the redemption of sinners by Christ*</u>.

Hebrews 8:13 In that he saith, A new *covenant*, he hath made the first old. Now that which decayeth and waxeth old *is* ready to vanish away.

Hebrews 9:1 Then verily the first *covenant* had also ordinances of divine service, and a worldly sanctuary.

Hebrews 9:11 – 13 11 But <u>Christ being come an high priest of good things to come</u>, by a greater and more perfect tabernacle, not made with hands, that is to say, not of this building; 12 Neither by the blood of goats and calves, <u>but by his own blood he entered in once into the holy place</u>, <u>having obtained eternal</u> <u>redemption *for us*</u>. 13 For if the blood of bulls and of goats, and the ashes of an heifer sprinkling the unclean, sanctifieth to the purifying of the flesh:

Hebrews 9:14 <u>How much more shall the blood of Christ</u>, who through the eternal Spirit offered himself without spot to God, <u>purge your conscience</u> from dead works <u>to serve the living God</u> ?

> <u>Conscience</u>, *n. [..., to know, to be privy to; ...]* **1.** *Internal or self-knowing, or judgment of right or wrong;* *or the faculty, power or principle within us, which decides* *on the lawfulness or unlawfulness of our own actions and* *affections, and instantly approves or condemns them.*
>
> Being convicted by their own conscience, they went out one by one. **John viii**

Hebrews 9:15 And for this cause <u>he is the mediator of the new testament</u>, that <u>by means of death</u>, <u>for the redemption of the transgressions *that were* under the first testament</u>, they which are called might receive the promise of eternal inheritance.

Hebrews 9:16 For where a <u>testament</u> *is*, there must also of necessity be the death of the <u>testator</u>. 17 For a testament *is* of force after men are dead: otherwise it is of no strength at all while the testator liveth. 18 Whereupon neither the first *testament* was dedicated without blood.

> <u>Testament</u>, *n. [..., to make a will.]* *1. A solemn authentic instrument in writing, by which a person declares his will as to the* *disposal of his estate and effects after his death. This is otherwise called a will.* *A testament, to be valid, must be made when the <u>testator</u> is of sound mind, and it must be subscribed,* *witnessed and published in such a manner as the law prescribes.*
>
> <u>Testator</u>, *n. A man who makes and leaves a will or testament at death.*

from : page 35

Gospel, *n. [Sax. godspell; god, good, and spell, history, relation, narration, word, speech, that which is uttered, announced, sent or communicated; answering to the Gr. ..., L. evangelium, a good or joyful message.]*
The history of the birth, life, actions, death, resurrection, ascension, and doctrines of Jesus Christ; or a revelation of the grace of God to fallen man through a mediator, including the character, actions, and doctrines of Christ, with the whole scheme of salvation, as revealed by Christ and his apostles. This gospel is said to have been preached to Abraham, by the promise, "in thee shall all nations be blessed." **Gal. iii. 8** .
It is called the gospel of God. **Rom. i. 1** .
It is called the gospel of Christ. **Rom. i. 16** .
It is called the gospel of salvation. **Eph. i. 13** .

from : page 37

Renew, *v.t. 1. To renovate ; to restore to a former state, or to a good state, after decay or depravation;*
8. In theology, to make new ; to renovate ; to transform ; to change from natural enmity to the love of God and his law ; to implant holy affections in the heart ; to regenerate.

from : page 41

Infidel, *n. One who disbelieves the inspiration of the Scriptures, and the divine origin of christianity*

My personal notes:

Christ came to serve

We are to serve one another in the love of Jesus, our LORD and SAVIOUR

HE always did the will of HIS FATHER!!!
continued...

My note: *The first covenant was made by the blood of an animal and the second covenant was made by the blood of the Lord Jesus Christ !!!*
By , prep. 3. Through , or with , denoting the agent, means, instrument or cause ;

Hebrews 9:27,28

27 And as it is appointed unto men once to die, but after this the judgment:
28 So Christ was once offered to bear the sins of many; and unto them that look for him
shall he appear the second time without sin unto salvation.

Hebrews 10:14 – 18
Read: **Jeremiah 31:27 – 34**

14 For by one offering he hath perfected for ever them that are sanctified.
15 *Whereof* the Holy Ghost also is a witness to us: for after that he had said before,
16 This *is* the covenant that I will make with them after those days, saith the Lord,
I will put my laws into their hearts, and in their minds will I write them;
17 And their sins and iniquities will I remember no more.
18 Now where remission of these *is*, *there is* no more offering for sin.

Hebrews 12:24 And to Jesus the mediator of the new covenant, and to the blood of sprinkling,
that speaketh better things than *that of* Abel.

Hebrews 13:20,21 20 Now the God of peace, that brought again from the dead our Lord Jesus, that great shepherd
of the sheep, through the blood of the everlasting covenant, 21 Make you perfect in
every good work to do his will, working in you that which is wellpleasing in his sight,
through Jesus Christ; to whom *be* glory for ever and ever. A-men'.

My note: **Genesis 6:18** *is the first reference to covenant, within the King James Version of the Holy Bible.*

My note: **Establish, is to fix firm and to continue.**

Genesis 6:17,18 17And, behold, I, even I, do bring a flood of waters upon the earth, to destroy all flesh, wherein *is* the breath of
life, from under heaven; *and* every thing that *is* in the earth shall die. 18 But with thee will I establish
my covenant; and thou shalt come into the ark, thou, and thy sons, and thy wife, and thy sons' wives with thee.

*Covenant, n. [... Literally, a coming together; a meeting or agreement of minds.] 3. In theology, ... The covenant of redemption,
is the mutual agreement between the Father and Son, respecting the redemption of sinners by Christ.*

My note: **Made, is to set forth or begin.**

Genesis 15:18 In the same day the LORD made a covenant with Abram, saying, Unto thy seed have I given this land,
from the river of Egypt unto the great river, the river Euphrates:

Genesis 17:7 And I will establish my covenant between me and thee and thy seed after thee in their generations
for an everlasting covenant, to be a God unto thee, and to thy seed after thee.

Genesis 17:21 But my covenant will I establish with Isaac. which Sarah shall bear unto thee at this set time in the next year.

10-5-16 @ 11:17am Wednesday

My note: *Noah had a mind of agreement towards the LORD in that, Noah willingly did as the LORD declared unto him so,
Noah's mind was continually in agreement unto the LORD's word. And, as the LORD spoke unto Noah about a
covenant, it was without question that Noah's mind was in agreement to the word of the LORD; which means Noah
willingly agreed to the LORD's word and thus, it is a covenant which is made by the LORD.*

My note: *Likewise, the covenant made with Abram / Abraham in that, Abram / Abraham sincerely desired to do
the will of the LORD; making the LORD's word a covenant however, it was broken by man ; so, it was not everlasting !*

My note: *And, ultimately, the covenant between the Father and the Son whereby, there is complete agreement as to
the salvation of the world and the redemption of man; which was to come since the fall of man, in the Garden of Eden
and this covenant was completely fulfilled with the obedience of Jesus Christ ! HIS desire was to do the will of
HIS Father, which is in heaven ! and is an everlasting covenant !!!*

Even so, come, Lord Jesus. **Revelation 22:20**

My personal notes:

Gifts of the Holy Spirit
We are to serve
continued...

Christ came to serve

We are to serve one another in the love of Jesus, our LORD and SAVIOUR

HE always did the will of HIS FATHER!!!
continued...

My note: *Jesus doing the will of HIS FATHER established those who receive HIM, as a child of God; who is now able to do the will of the Father and of the Lord Jesus Christ, by the power of the Holy Ghost; which dwelleth in us!*

We serve our Lord Jesus Christ by serving others, in the love and power of the Holy Spirit; proclaiming Jesus Christ, as both LORD and SAVIOUR, all to the glory of God the Father.

John 14:23   Jesus answered and said unto him, **If a man love me, he will keep my words: and my Father will love him, and we will come unto him, and make our abode with him.**

My note: **John 15:14** *is specifically for HIS disciples. Read:* **John 13:34,35 – 18:1**   **_My note_**: *However, this applies to all the children of God.*

John 15:12,13,14   **12 This is my commandment, That ye love one another, as I have loved you.**
13 Greater love hath no man than this, that a man lay down his life for his friends.
14 Ye are my friends, if ye do whatsoever I command you.

My note: *Paul's example is our focus also!* vs. 20 & 21

Acts 20:18 – 21   **18** And when they were come to him, he said unto them, Ye know, from the first day that I came into Asia, after what manner I have been with you at all seasons. **19** Serving the Lord with all humility of mind, and with many tears, and temptations, which befell me by the lying in wait of the Jews: **20** *And* how I kept back nothing that was profitable *unto you*, but have shewed you, and have taught you publickly, and from house to house, **21** Testifying both to the Jews, and also to the Greeks, repentance toward God, and faith toward our Lord Jesus Christ.

Romans 12:9 – 21   **9** *Let* love be without dissimulation. Abhor that which is evil; cleave to that which is good.
Read: 12:1 – 21   **10** *Be* kindly affectioned one to another with brotherly love; in honour preferring one another; **11** Not slothful in business; fervent in spirit; serving the Lord; **12** Rejoicing in hope; patient in tribulation; continuing instant in prayer; **13** Distributing to the necessity of saints; given to hospitality. **14** Bless them which persecute you: bless, and curse not. **15** Rejoice with them that do rejoice, and weep with them that weep. **16** *Be* of the same mind one toward another. Mind not high things, but condescend to men of low estate. Be not wise in your own conceits. **17** Recompense to no man evil for evil. Provide things honest in the sight of all men. **18** If it be possible, as much as lieth in you, live peaceably with all men. **19** Dearly beloved, avenge not yourselves, but *rather* give place unto wrath: for it is written, Vengeance *is* mine; I will repay, saith the Lord. **20** Therefore if thine enemy hunger, feed him; if he thirst, give him drink: for in so doing thou shalt heap coals of fire on his head. **21** Be not overcome of evil, but overcome evil with good.

My note: In **Romans 12:19,** "avenge" *is used in the sense that the man of God is not to retaliate or to return evil for evil, in the same manner in which it is given ; with a hateful or spiteful or prideful or, ... heart.*

My note: *"coals of fire upon his head" is a quote from* **Proverbs 25:21,22**
My note: *"coals of fire upon his head" – (inflames the conscience); (stirs the conscience of God's goodness and HIS wrath, as being ever present):* " for it is written, Vengeance is mine; I will repay, saith the Lord."
Deuteronomy 32:35

Dissimulation, *n. [..., to make like; like.] The act of dissembling;* a hiding under a false appearance; *a* feigning; *false pretension; hypocrisy. Dissimulation may be simply concealment of the opinions, sentiments or purpose; but it includes also the assuming of a false or counterfeit appearance which conceals the real opinions or purpose.*

Feigning, *ppr. Imagining; inventing; pretending;* making a false show.

Gifts of the Holy Spirit
We are to serve
continued...

Christ came to serve

We are to serve one another in the love of Jesus, our LORD and SAVIOUR

HE always did the will of HIS FATHER!!!

<u>Romans 12:9-21</u> *continued...*   *continued...*

<u>**Abhor**</u>, *v.t.* [*... to shiver or shake; to look terrible.*] *3. <u>To cast off or reject</u>.*   **Psalm lxxxix . 38**   Psalm 89:38

<u>**Cleave**</u>, *v.i.* *1. To stick; <u>to adhere; to hold to</u>.*   Cleave to that which is good. **Romans xii** .

<u>**Kindly**</u>, *adv. With good will; with a disposition to make others happy or to oblige; benevolently; favorably.*   **Rom. xii** .

<u>**Affectioned**</u>, *a. 1. <u>Disposed</u> ; having an affection of heart .*   Be ye kindly affectioned one to another. **Rom xii**

> **Disposed**, *pp. bestowed*   **Bestowed**, *ppr. Given <u>gratuitously</u> ; deposited for safe-keeping.*
> <u>**Gratuitously**</u>, *adv. Freely; voluntarily ; without claim or merit ; without an equivalent or compensation ;*
> *as labor or service gratuitously bestowed.*

Affectioned → *Disposed* → *Given Gratuitously* → *freely given* → *etc.*   (<u>My note</u>: *having a gratuitous of heart*)

<u>**Honour**</u>, *n.*
<u>Honor</u>, *n. 1. The esteem due or paid to worth ; high estimation .*   (<u>My note</u>: *For Christ's sake.*)

<u>My note</u>: **one**
<u>**Preferring**</u>, *ppr. Regarding above others ; advancing ^ to a higher station ;*   <u>My note</u>: *being favorably attentive to*

<u>**Slothful**</u>, *a. Inactive ; sluggish ; lazy ; indolent ; idle .*   He that is <u>slothful</u> in his work, is brother to him that is a great waster. **Prov. xviii** .

<u>**Fervent**</u>, *a. [... to be hot, to boil, to glow ...] 3. <u>Ardent</u> ; very warm; earnest; excited; animated; glowing; as fervent zeal.*
<u>Fervent</u> in spirit. **Rom. xii** .
> <u>Ardent</u> , *a. 3. Warm, applied to the passions and affections; passionate; affectionate; much engaged; <u>zealous</u>*
> **Zealous, a.** *Warmly engaged*

<u>**Hospitality**</u>, *n. The act or practice of receiving and entertaining strangers or guests without reward ...*

<u>**Condescend**</u>, *v.i. 1. To descend from the privileges of superior rank or dignity, to do some act to an inferior, which strict justice*
or the ordinary rules of civility do not require. Hence, to subject or yield, as to an inferior,
implying an occasional relinquishment of distinction.
Mind not high things, but <u>condescend</u> to men of low estate. **Rom. xii** .

<u>**Conceit**</u>, *n. [to take or seize.] 1. Conception; that which is conceived, imagined, or formed in the mind; idea; thought; image.*
6. Favorable or self-flattering opinion; a lofty or vain conception of ones own person or
accomplishments.

<u>**Recompense**</u>, *v.t. 2. To require; to repay; to return an equivalent; in a bad sense.*   Recompense to no man evil for evil. **Rom. xii** .

<u>**Avenge**</u>, *v.t. 1. To vindicate by inflicting pain or evil on the wrong doer.*
> <u>My note</u>: *<u>Avenge</u> is being used to distinguish the difference between man's satisfaction of returning evil for evil*
> *and God's <u>vengeance</u>, which is perfect justice! Likewise, when God <u>avenges</u>, HIS justice is perfect!*

> <u>**Retaliate**</u>, *v.t. <u>To return like for like</u>; to repay or requite by an act of the same kind as has been received.*

<u>Strong's Concordance</u> <u>Avenge</u> *...* **Romans 12:19** *1556* → *<u>Strong's Greek Dictionary of the New Testament</u> 1556 to vindicate, <u>retaliate</u>,*

<u>**Vengeance**</u>, *n. <u>The infliction of pain on another, in return for an injury or offense</u>. Such infliction, when it proceeds from malice*
or mere resentment, and is not necessary for the purposes of justice, is <u>revenge</u>, and a most <u>hainous</u> crime.
<u>*When such infliction proceeds from a mere love of justice, and the necessity of punishing offenders for the*</u>
<u>*support of the laws, it is vengeance, and is warrantable and just. In this case, vengeance is a just retribution,*</u>
<u>*recompense or punishment. In this latter sense the word is used in Scripture, and frequently applied to the*</u>
<u>*punishments inflicted by God on sinners.*</u>
To me belongeth vengeance and recompense. **Deut. xxxii : 35**
The Lord will take vengeance on his adversaries. **Nah. i**

<u>**Revenge**</u>, *n. 1. Return of an injury; the deliberate infliction of pain or injury on a person in return*
for an injury received from him. Milton. Dryden.

<u>**Hainous**</u>, *a. Properly, hateful; <u>odious</u>.*   **Odious**, *a. <u>Deserving of hatred</u>.*

Gifts of the Holy Spirit
We are to serve
continued...

Christ came to serve

We are to serve one another in the love of Jesus, our LORD and SAVIOUR.

HE always did the will of HIS FATHER!!!
continued...

Philippians 2:1,2 1 If *there be* therefore any consolation in Christ, if any comfort of love, if any fellowship of the
Read: 2:1 – 18   Spirit, if any bowels and mercies, 2 Fulfil ye my joy, that ye be likeminded,
having the same love, *being* of one accord, of one mind.

Philippians 2:5 – 8 5 Let this mind be in you, which was also in Christ Jesus: 6 Who, being in the form of God, thought it not
robbery to be equal with God: 7 But made himself of no reputation, and took upon him the form of
a servant, and was made in the likeness of men: 8 And being found in fashion as a man,
he humbled himself, and became obedient unto death, even the death of the cross.

Philippians 2:13 For it is God which worketh in you both to will and to do of *his* good pleasure.

Philippians 2:17 Yea, and if I be offered upon the sacrifice and service of your faith, I joy, and rejoice with you all.

Galatians 5:13,14 13 For, brethren, ye have been called unto liberty; only *use* not liberty for an occasion to the flesh,
but by love serve one another. 14 For all the law is fulfilled in one word, *even* in this;
Thou shalt love thy neighbour as thyself.

Ephesians 5:1,2 1 Be ye therefore followers of God, as dear children; 2 And walk in love, as Christ also hath loved
us, and hath given himself for us an offering and a sacrifice to God for a sweetsmelling savour.

1John3:17 But whoso hath this world's good, and seeth his brother have need, and shutteth up his bowels *of*
compassion from him, how dwelleth the love of God in him? 18 My little children,
let us not love in word, neither in tongue; but in deed and in truth.

James 2:26 For as the body without the spirit is dead, so faith without works is dead also.

1John 4:21 And this commandment have we from him, That he who loveth God love his brother also.

1Thessalonians 3:12 And the Lord make you to increase and abound in love one toward another,
and toward all *men*, even as we *do* toward you:

1Thessalonians 4:9,10 9 But as touching brotherly love ye need not that I write unto you: for ye yourselves are
taught of God to love one another. 10 And indeed ye do it toward all the brethren which
are in all Macedonia: but we beseech you, brethren, that ye increase more and more;

Luke 22:25 – 27 25 And he said unto them, The kings of the Gentiles exercise lordship over them; and they that exercise
authority upon them are called benefactors. 26 But ye *shall* not *be* so: but he that is greatest
among you, let him be as the younger; and he that is chief, as he that doth serve. 27 For
whether *is* greater, he that sitteth at meat, or he that serveth? *is* not he that sitteth at meat?
but I am among you as he that serveth.

Serving God, through our Lord Jesus Christ, by the power of the Holy Spirit
is
glorious and heavenly!

The Lord being served in heaven!!!

Revelation 7:15 Therefore are they before the throne of God, and serve him day and night in his temple:
Read: 7:9 – 17   and he that sitteth on the throne shall dwell among them.

Revelation 22:3 And there shall be no more curse: but the throne of God and of the Lamb shall be in it;
Read: 22:1 – 21   and his servants shall serve him:

My personal notes:

Gifts of the Holy Spirit
We are to serve
continued...

Christ came to serve

We are to serve one another in the love of Jesus, our LORD and SAVIOUR.

HE always did the will of HIS FATHER!!!
continued...

Ephesians 4:11 – 14   11 And he gave some, apostles; and some, prophets; and some, evangelists;
and some, pastors and teachers; 12 For the perfecting of the saints,
for the work of the ministry, <u>for the edifying of the body of Christ</u>:

James 2:14 – 18   14 What d*oth it* profit, my brethren, though a man say he hath faith, and have not works? can faith save him?
Read: 1:1 – 2:26   15 If a brother or sister be naked, and destitute of daily food, 16 And one of you say unto them, Depart in
peace, be *ye* warmed and filled; notwithstanding ye give them not those things which are needful to the body;
what *doth it* profit? 17 Even so faith, if it hath not works, is dead, being alone. 18 Yea, a man may say,
Thou hast faith, and I have works: shew me thy faith without thy works, and
<u>I will shew thee my faith by my works.</u>

2Thessalonians 2:16,17   16 Now our Lord Jesus Christ himself, and God, even our Father, which hath loved us,
and hath given *us* everlasting consolation and good hope through grace,
17 Comfort your hearts, and stablish you <u>in every good word and work.</u>

1Peter 1:22,23   22 Seeing ye have purified your souls in obeying the truth through the Spirit unto unfeigned love of
the brethren, *see that ye* <u>love one another</u> with a pure heart fervently: 23 <u>Being born again</u>, not of
corruptible seed, but of incorruptible, <u>by the word of God</u>, which liveth and abideth for ever.

Purified

Purify, v.t. [..., pure, and ..., to make.]   3. To free from guilt or the defilement of sin; as, to purify the heart.
Who gave himself for us, that he might redeem us from all iniquity, and *purify*
to himself a peculiar people, zealous of good works. **Tit. ii** .

Unfeigned, *a.   Not feigned; not counterfeit; not hypocritical; real; sincere; as unfeigned piety to God; unfeigned love to man.*

Feign, v.t. 2. To make a show of; to pretend; to assume a false appearance; to counterfeit.

Pure, *a.   3. Genuine; real; true; incorrupt; unadulterated; as pure religion.* **James i** .
12. Mere; <u>absolute</u>; that and that only; unconnectd with any thing else;
<u>Absolute</u>, a. 1. Literally, in a general sense, free, independent of any thing extraneous.

Heart, *n. 4. The seat of the affections and passions, as of love, joy, grief, enmity, courage, pleasure, &c.*

Fervently, *adv. Earnestly; eagerly; vehemently; with great warmth.*

Fervent, a. [..., to be hot, to boil, to glow; ...] 3. <u>Ardent</u>; very warm; earnest; excited; animated; glowing   Fervent in spirit. **Rom. xii** .

<u>Ardent</u>, a. 3. Warm, applied to the passions and affections; passionate; affectionate;
much engaged; zealous;

1Peter 1:23 "being born again" "by the word of God" ; **Matthew 6:9** Our Father which art in heaven, Hallowed be thy name.

Romans 8:14 ,15   14 For as many as are led by the Spirit of God, <u>they are the sons of God</u>. 15 For ye have not received the
Read: 8:16, 17   spirit of bondage again to fear; but <u>ye have received the Spirit of adoption, whereby we cry</u>, Abba, Father.

My personal note: Even naturally with man, within a natural father, there is a joy and honorable pride with the conception of,
the nurturing and growth within the mother, and the physical birth of his child.
Man is created in the image of the LORD God, our Father and Creator.

Genesis 1:26,27   26 And God said, Let us make man in our image, after our likeness: ...
27 So <u>God created man in his *own* image</u>, in the image of God created he him; male and female created he them.

Genesis 4:25   And Adam knew his wife again; and she bare a son, and called his name Seth: For God, *said she*, hath appointed
me another seed instead of Abel, whom Cain slew.

Genesis 5:1 – 3   1 This *is* the book of the generations of Adam. In the day that God created man, in the likeness of God made he him;
2 Male and female created he them; and blessed them, and called their name Adam, in the day when they were created.
3 And Adam lived an hundred and thirty years, and begat *a son* in his own likeness, after his image; and called his name Seth:

The Filling of the Holy Ghost

My note:
Being filled, means to be under the influence of the Holy Ghost; yielding unto Him and not resisting HIM.

Luke 4:1 And Jesus being full of the Holy Ghost returned from Jordan, and was led by the Spirit into the wilderness.

My note:
I do not have more of the Holy Spirit, the Holy Spirit has more of me!
I am more sensitive unto HIM and I desire to do HIS will; the will of God my Father, in Jesus Christ my Lord and Saviour.
I am yielding more and more unto HIM, instead of resisting HIM.
As with being drunk with wine, we have less resistance abiding within us.

Ephesians 5:18
And be not drunk with wine, wherein is excess; but be filled with the Spirit;

My note: Being filled is being compared with being drunk with wine.

Drunk, *a. overwhelmed or overpowered by spirituous liquor*   *My note: under the influence of*
Filled, *pp. Made full; supplied with abundance.*

Fill, *v.t. [... to thrust or drive, ...] Properly, to press ; to crowd ; to stuff.   Hence, to put or pour in, till the thing will hold no more;*

Ephesians 5:17 – 21   16 Redeeming the time, because the days are evil. 17 Wherefore be ye not unwise, but understanding what the will of the Lord *is*. 18 And be not drunk with wine, wherein is excess; but be filled with the Spirit; 19 Speaking to yourselves in psalms and hymns and spiritual songs, singing and making melody in your heart to the Lord; 20 Giving thanks always for all things unto God and the Father in the name of the Lord Jesus Christ; 21 Submitting yourselves one to another in the fear of God.

Acts 1:16 Men *and* brethren, this scripture must needs have been fulfilled, which the Holy Ghost by the mouth of David spake before concerning Judas, which was guide to them that took Jesus.

Acts 2:4 And they were all filled with the Holy Ghost, and began to speak with other tongues,
as the Spirit gave them utterance.

Acts 6:8 And Stephen, full of faith and power, did great wonders and miracles among the people.

Acts 7:55 But he, being full of the Holy Ghost, looked up stedfastly into heaven, and saw the glory of God,
and Jesus standing on the right hand of God,

Acts 7:59 And they stoned Stephen, calling upon *God*, and saying, Lord Jesus, receive my spirit.

Blessings with being filled with the Holy Ghost

He leads and he guides

Romans 8:14   For as many as are led by the Spirit of God, they are the sons of God.

Psalm 143:10 Teach me to do thy will; for thou *art* my God: thy spirit *is* good; lead me into the land of uprightness.

Revelation 2:7   He that hath an ear, let him hear what the Spirit saith unto the churches; To them that overcometh
will I grant to eat of the tree of life, which is in the midst of the paradise of God.

Revelation 22:17 And the Spirit and the bride say, Come. And let him that heareth say, come. And let him that is athirst come.
And whosoever will, let him take the water of life freely.

Psalm 23:2,3   1 The LORD *is* my shepherd; I shall not want. 2 He maketh me to lie down in green pastures: he leadeth me
Read: **23:1 – 6**   beside the still waters. 3 He restoreth my soul: he leadeth me in the paths of righteousness for his name's sake.

John 16:13   Howbeit when he, the Spirit of truth, is come, he will guide you into all truth: for he shall not speak of
himself; but whatsoever he shall hear, *that* shall he speak: and he will shew you things to come.

Psalm 31:1 - 3   1 In thee, O LORD, do I put my trust; let me never be ashamed: deliver me in thy righteousness.
2 Bow down thine ear to me; deliver me speedily: be thou my strong rock, for an house of defence to save me.
3 For thou *art* my rock and my fortress: therefore for thy name's sake lead me, and guide me.

Psalm 25:9 The meek will he guide in judgment: and the meek will he teach his way.   *Read:* Psalm 25:1 – 21

Psalm 73:24 Thou shalt guide me with thy counsel, and afterward receive me *to* glory.   *Read:* Psalm 73:1 – 28

Romans 8:9 But ye are not in the flesh, but in the Spirit, if so be that the Spirit of God dwell in you.
Now if any man have not the Spirit of Christ, he is none of his.

My personal notes:

He is the Spirit of truth

John 14:16,17   16 And I will pray the Father, and he shall give you another Comforter, that he may abide with you for ever; 17 *Even* **the Spirit of truth**; whom the world cannot receive, because it seeth him not, neither knoweth him: but ye know him; for he dwelleth with you, and shall be in you.

John 15:26 But when the Comforter is come, whom I will send unto you from the Father, *even* **the Spirit of truth**, which proceedeth from the Father, he shall testify of me:

> **Proceedeth**, *v.i.*
> Procede, *v.i.* **4.** *To come from a person or place.*
>
> **John 8:42** Jesus said unto them, If God were your Father, ye would love me: for I proceeded forth and came from God; neither came I of myself, but he sent me.

1John 5:4 – 6 4 For whatsoever is born of God overcometh the world: and this is the victory that overcometh the world, *even* our faith. 5 Who is he that overcometh the world, but he that believeth that Jesus is the Son of God? 6 This is he that came by water and blood, *even* Jesus Christ; not by water only, but by water and blood. And it is the Spirit that beareth witness, because the Sprit is truth.

John 16:7 – 15 7 Nevertheless I tell you the truth; It is expedient for you that I go away: for if I go not away, the Comforter will not come unto you; but if I depart, I will send him unto you. 8 And when he is come, he will reprove the world of sin, and of righteousness, and of judgment: 9 Of sin, because they believe not on me; 10 Of righteousness, because I go to my Father, and ye see me no more; 11 Of judgment, because the prince of this world is judged. 12 I have yet many things to say unto you, but ye cannot bear them now. 13 Howbeit when he, **the Spirit of truth**, is come, he will guide you into all truth: for he shall not speak of himself; but whatsoever he shall hear, *that* shall he speak: and he will shew you things to come. 14 He shall glorify me: for he shall receive of mine, and shall shew *it* unto you. 15 All things that the Father hath are mine: therefore said I, that he shall take of mine, and shall shew *it* unto you.

He teaches

John 14:26   But the Comforter, *which is* the Holy Ghost, whom the Father will send in my name, he shall teach you all things, and bring all things to your remembrance, whatsoever I have said unto you.

Luke 12:12   For the Holy Ghost shall teach you in the same hour what ye ought to say.

1Corinthians 2:13 Which things also we speak, not in the words which man's wisdom teacheth, but which the Holy Ghost teacheth; comparing spiritual things with spiritual.

1John 2:27 But the anointing which ye have received of him abideth in you, and ye need not that any man teach you: but as the same anointing teacheth you of all things, as is truth, and is no lie, and even as it hath taught you, ye shall abide in him.

Psalm 143:10 Teach me to do thy will; for thou *art* my God: thy spirit *is* good; lead me into the land of uprightness.

Psalm 25:9 The meek will he guide in judgment: and the meek will he teach his way.
Read: 25:1 – 21

54

He is the Comforter and He comforts

John 14:16 And I will pray the Father, and he shall give you another Comforter, that he may abide with you for ever;

John 14:26 But the Comforter, *which is* the Holy Ghost, whom the Father will send in my name, he shall teach you all things, and bring all things to your remembrance, whatsoever I have said unto you.

John 15:26 But when the Comforter is come, whom I will send unto you from the Father, *even* the Spirit of truth, which proceedeth from the Father, he shall testify of me:

John 16:7 Nevertheless I tell you the truth; It is expedient for you that I go away: for if I go not away, the Comforter will not come unto you; but if I depart, I will send him unto you.

Expedient, a. **2.** *Useful; profitable.*

Acts 9:31 Then had the churches rest throughout all Judaea and Galilee and Samaria, and were edified; and walking in the fear of the Lord, and in the comfort of the Holy Ghost, were multiplied.

Philippians 2:1,2 **1** If *there be* therefore any consolation in Christ, if any comfort of love, if any fellowship of the Spirit, if any bowels of mercies, **2** Fulfil ye my joy, that ye be likeminded, having the same love, *being* of one accord, of one mind.

He helps us

Romans 8:26 Likewise the Spirit also helpeth our infirmities: for we know not what we should pray for as we ought:
Read: 8:22 – 39   but the Spirit itself maketh intercession for us with groanings which cannot be uttered. **27** And he that searcheth the hearts knoweth what *is* the mind of the Spirit, because he maketh intercession for the saints according to *the will of* God. **28** And we know that all things work together for good to them that love God, to them who are called according to *his* purpose.

Infirmity, n. **2.** *Weakness of mind; failing; fault.*

My note: Very comforting!!! **Intercession**, n. *The act of interceding ; mediation ; interposition between parties at variance, with a view to reconciliation; prayer of solicitation to one party in favor of another.*

Hebrews 4:14 – 16   **14** Seeing then that we have a great high priest, that is passed into the heavens, Jesus the Son of God, let us hold fast *our* profession. **15** For we have not an high priest which cannot be touched with the feeling of our infirmities; but was in all points tempted like as *we are, yet* without sin. **16** Let us therefore come boldly unto the throne of grace, that we may obtain mercy, and find grace to help in time of need.

Hebrews 13:5,6 **1** Let brotherly love continue.
5 *Let your* conversation *be* without covetousness; *and be* content with such things as ye have: for he hath said, I will never leave thee, nor forsake thee. **6** So that we may boldly say, The Lord *is* my helper, and I will not fear what man shall do unto me.

Psalm 33:18 – 22 **18** Behold, the eye of the LORD *is* upon them that fear him, upon them that hope in his mercy; **19** To deliver their soul from death, and to keep them alive in famine. **20** Our soul waiteth for the LORD: he *is* our help and our shield. **21** For our heart shall rejoice in him, because we have trusted in his holy name. **22** Let thy mercy, O LORD, be upon us, according as we hope in thee.

Read: 2Corinthians 7:6,7 *and* 1Corinthians 1:1 – 5

He gives us His peace

Philippians 4:4 – 8   **4** Rejoice in the Lord alway: *and* again I say, Rejoice. **5** Let your moderation be known unto all men. The Lord *is* at hand. **6** Be careful for nothing; but in every thing by prayer and supplication with thanksgiving let your requests be made known unto God. **7** And the peace of God, which passeth all understanding, shall keep your hearts and minds through Christ Jesus. **8** Finally, brethren, whatsoever things are true, whatsoever things *are* honest, whatsoever things *are* just, whatsoever things *are* pure, whatsoever things *are* lovely, whatsoever things *are* of good report; if *there be* any virtue, and if *there be* any praise, think on these things.

My personal notes:

He gives us hope and joy and peace

Romans 15:13   Now the God of hope fill you with all joy and peace in believing,
that ye may abound in hope, through the power of the Holy Ghost.

Romans 5:1   Therefore being justified by faith, we have peace with God through our Lord Jesus Christ:

Romans 14:17 – 19   **17** For the kingdom of God is not meat and drink; but righteousness, and peace, and joy
Read: 14:1 - 23   in the Holy Ghost. **18** For he that in these things serveth Christ *is* acceptable to God,
and approved of men. **19** Let us therefore follow after the things which make for peace,
and things wherewith one may edify another.

John 15:8 – 13   **8 Herein is my Father glorified, that ye bear much fruit; so shall ye be my disciples.**
Read: 10:31 – 11:27   **9 As the Father hath loved me, so have I loved you: continue ye in my love.**
10 If ye keep my commandments, ye shall abide in my love; even as I have kept my Father's
commandments, and abide in his love. 11 These things have I spoken unto you, that my joy
might remain in you, and *that* your joy might be full. 12 This is my commandment, That ye
love one another, as I have loved you. 13 Greater love hath no man than this, that a man lay
down his life for his friends. 14 Ye are my friends, if ye do whatsoever I command you.

Hebrews 12:1,2   **1** Wherefore seeing we also are compassed about with so great a cloud of witnesses, let us lay aside every
weight, and the sin which doth so easily beset *us*, and let us run with patience the race that is set before us,
2 Looking unto Jesus the author and finisher of *our* faith; who for the joy that was set before him
endured the cross, despising the shame, and is set down at the right hand of the throne of God.

Colossians 1:26,27   **26** *Even* the mystery which hath been hid from ages and from generations, but now is made
manifest to his saints: **27** To whom God would make known what *is* the riches of the glory
of this mystery among the Gentiles; which is Christ in you, the hope of glory:

Psalm 33:18 – 22   **18** Behold, the eye of the LORD *is* upon them that fear him, upon them that hope in his mercy; **19** To deliver
their soul from death, and to keep them alive in famine. **20** Our soul waiteth for the LORD: he *is* our help
and our shield. **21** For our heart shall rejoice in him, because we have trusted in his holy name.
22 Let thy mercy, O LORD, be upon us, according as we hope in thee.

1Thessalonians 1:1 – 6   **1** Paul, and Silvanus, and Timotheus, unto the church of the Thessalonians *which is* in
Read: 1:1 – 2:20   God the Father and *in* the Lord Jesus Christ: Grace *be* unto you, and peace, from God
our Father, and the Lord Jesus Christ. **2** We give thanks to God always for you all,
making mention of you in our prayers; **3** Remembering without ceasing your work of
faith, and labour of love, and patience of hope in our Lord Jesus Christ, in the sight of
God our Father; **4** Knowing, brethren beloved, your election of God. **5** For our gospel
came not unto you in word only, but also in power, and in the Holy Ghost, and in much
assurance; as ye know what manner of men we were among you for your sake. **6** And
ye became followers of us, and of the Lord, having received the word in much affliction,
with joy of the Holy Ghost:

Galatians 5:22 – 26   **22** But the fruit of the Spirit is love, joy, peace, longsuffering, gentleness, goodness, faith,
23 Meekness, temperance: against such there is no law. **24** And they that are Christ's
have crucified the flesh with the affections and lusts. **25** If we live in the Spirit, let us
also walk in the Spirit. **26** Let us not be desirous of vain glory, provoking one another,
envying one another.

Romans 8:6   For to be carnally minded *is* death; but to be spiritually minded *is* life and peace.
Read: 8:1 – 39

Romans 9:26   And it shall come to pass, *that* in the place where it was said unto them, Ye *are* not my people;
there shall they be called the children of the living God.

He gives us hope and joy and peace
continued...

Romans 15:13

Hope, n. 2. *Confidence in a future event; the highest degree of well founded expectation of good;*

Joy, n. [..., to *rejoice*; ...] 1. *The passion or emotion excited by the acquisition or expectation of good;*
4. *A glorious and triumphant state.*
Who for the joy that was set before him, endured the cross. **Heb. xii** .

Rejoice, v.i. [... *But it is easy to see that the primary sense is to shout, or to be animated or excited.*]

Peace, n. 6. *Harmony; concord; a sense of reconciliation between parties at variance.*

Harmony, n. [... *a setting together, a closure or seam, agreement, ...*] 3. *Concord; agreement; accordance in facts;*
as the harmony of the gospels.

Concord, n. [... , *the heart. See Accord.*] 1. *Agreement between persons; ...*
Agreement, n. *concord ; harmony ; conformity .*

Reconciliation, n. 1. *The act of reconciling parties at variance; renewal of friendship after disagreement or enmity.*
2. *In Scripture, the means by which sinners are reconciled and brought into a state of favor*
with God, after natural estrangement or enmity; the atonement; expiation.

Reconcile, v.t. [... *The literal sense is to call back into union.*] *My note: The Union in believing God and yielding unto HIM.*

Hope, n. [... *The primary sense is to extend, to reach forward.*] 1. *A desire of some good, accompanied with at least a*
slight expectation of obtaining it, or a belief that it is obtainable. Hope therefore always gives
pleasure or joy; whereas wish and desire may produce or be accompanied with pain or anxiety.

Romans 5:1   *and*   Romans 8:30 Moreover whom he did predestinate, them he also called: and whom he called,
them he also justified: and whom he justified, them he also glorified. 31 What shall we
then say to these things? If God be for us, who can be against us?

Justified, *My note: Pardoned and cleared from guilt.*
Justify, v.t. [... *just, and ..., to make.*] 2. *In theology, to pardon and clear from guilt; to absolve or acquit from*
guilt and merited punishment, and to accept as righteous on account of the
merits of the Savior, or by the application of Christ's atonement
to the offender. St. Paul.

Merited, pp. *Earned; deserved.*
Merit, n. [... *to earn or deserve ...*] *Desert; goodness or excellence which entitles one to honor or reward;*
any performance or worth which claims regard or compensation; thus we speak of the inability of
men to obtain salvation by their own merits.

Glorified, pp. *Honored ; dignified ; exalted to glory.*
Glory, n. 6. *The felicity of heaven prepared for the children of God; celestial bliss.*
Thou shalt guide me with thy counsel, and afterwards receive me to glory. **Ps. lxxiii** .

Felicity, n. 1. *Happiness, or rather great happiness : blessedness ; blissfulness ; appropriately, the joys of heaven.*

Romans 8:6 → Romans 8:16,17 16 The Spirit itself beareth witness with our spirit, that we are the children of God:
17 And if children, then heirs; heirs of God, and joint-heirs with Christ;
if so be that we suffer with *him*, that we may be also glorified together.

My note: "heirs of God" → *to receive eternal life and to receive a glorified body, as did Jesus Christ!*
My note: "joint-heirs with Christ;" → *everlasting life with God in heaven!*
My note: "if so be that we suffer with him," → *suffer the reproach of Christ!*

My note: The Lord Jesus Christ was rejected for who HE was/is ; the Son of the living God ; God manifest in the flesh ; the Saviour of the world.

Heir, n. 4. *One who is entitled to possess. In Scripture, saints are called heirs of the promise, heirs of righteousness,*
heirs of salvation, &c. , by virtue of the death of Christ, or of God's gracious promises.

Entitled, pp. *Dignified or distinguished by a title; having a claim;*
Title, n. 6. *Right ; or that which constitutes a just cause of exclusive possession;*
Right, n. 10. *Just claim ; immunity ; privilege.*
Privilege, n. 2. *Any peculiar benefit or advantage , right or immunity, not common to others of the human race.*

My note: All who are HIS children shall suffer ; the suffering is the persecution of confessing to be a child of the living God;
confessing to be a Christian who is worthy of heaven, according to the merit of our LORD & SAVIOUR JESUS CHRIST !!!

He sanctifies us

Romans 15:16   That I should be the minister of Jesus Christ to the Gentiles, ministering the gospel
of God, that the offering up of the Gentiles might be acceptable, being sanctified
by the Holy Ghost.

Sanctify, v.t. [..., holy, ..., to make.] 1. In a general sense, to cleanse, purify, or make holy. Addison.
Sanctified, *pp.   1. Made holy; consecrated; set apart for sacred service.*

1Peter 3:15   But sanctify the Lord God in your hearts: and *be* ready always to *give* an answer to every man that
asketh you a reason of the hope that is in you with meekness and fear:

He dwells in us / within each believer

1Corinthians 6:19, 20   19 What? know ye not that your body is the temple of the Holy Ghost *which is* in you,
which ye have of God, and ye are not your own? 20 For ye are bought with a price:
therefore glorify God in your body, and in your spirit, which are God's.

1John 3:1 – 3   1 Behold, what manner of love the Father hath bestowed upon us, that we should be called the
sons of God: therefore the world knoweth us not, because it knew him not. 2 Beloved, now are
we the sons of God, and it doth not yet appear what we shall be: but we know that, when he shall
appear, we shall be like him; for we shall see him as he is. 3 And every man that hath this hope in
him purifieth himself, even as he is pure.

1John 3:23, 24   23 And this is his commandment, That we should believe on the name of his Son Jesus Christ,
and love one another, as he gave us commandment.
24 And he that keepeth his commandments dwelleth in him, and he in him.
And hereby we know that he abideth in us, by the Spirit which he hath given us.

1John 4:13   Hereby know we that we dwell in him, and he in us, because he hath given us of his Spirit.

1John 5:20   And we know that the Son of God is come, and hath given us an understanding, that we may know him
that is true, and we are in him that is true, *even* in his Son Jesus Christ. This is the true God, and eternal life.

Romans 8:9 – 11   9 But ye are not in the flesh, but in the Spirit, if so be that the Spirit of God dwell in you.
Now if any man have not the Spirit of Christ, he is none of his. 10 And if Christ *be* in you,
the body *is* dead because of sin; but the Spirit *is* life because of righteousness. 11 But if
the Spirit of him that raised up Jesus from the dead dwell in you, he that raised up Christ
from the dead shall also quicken your mortal bodies by his Spirit that dwelleth in you.

2Timothy 1:14   That good thing which was committed unto thee keep by the Holy Ghost which dwelleth in us.
Read: 1:1 – 14   *My note:* "That good thing" *is* vs. 8 "the testimony of our Lord," "the gospel" *with* vs. 10 "through the gospel:"

Ephesians 1:1,2   1 Paul, an apostle of Jesus Christ by the will of God, to the saints which are at Ephesus, and to the faithful in
Christ Jesus: 2 Grace *be* to you, and peace, from God our Father, and *from* the Lord Jesus Christ.

Ephesians 1:7   In whom we have redemption through his blood, the forgiveness of sins, according to the riches of his grace;

Ephesians 2:8,9   8 For by grace are ye saved through faith; and that not of yourselves: *it is* the gift of God: 9 Not of works,
lest any man should boast.

Read: **Ephesians 1:1 – 2:22**

My note: The mind cannot comprehend this, but the Holy Spirit leads, guides and teaches us in all truth; that this is absolute truth.

*My note: These are great verses to share / declare with someone who focuses on his own works to please God unto salvation
and him being worthy of heaven ; instead of completely trusting in the Lord Jesus Christ unto salvation.*

John 19:30   When Jesus therefore had received the vinegar, he said, It is finished: and he bowed his head, and gave up the ghost.

<u>*My personal notes:*</u>

He seals us

Ephesians 1:13 – 18   13 In whom ye also *trusted*, after that ye heard the word of truth, the gospel of your salvation: in whom also after that ye believed, ye were sealed with that holy Spirit of promise, 14 Which is the earnest of our inheritance until the redemption of the purchased possession, unto the praise of his glory. 15 Wherefore I also, after I heard of your faith in the Lord Jesus, and love unto all the saints, 16 Cease not to give thanks for you, making mention of you in my prayers; 17 That the God of our Lord Jesus Christ, the Father of glory, may give unto you the spirit of wisdom and revelation in the knowledge of him: 18 The eyes of your understanding being enlightened; that ye may know what is the hope of his calling, and what the riches of the glory of his inheritance in the saints, 19 And what *is* the exceeding greatness of his power to us-ward who believe, according to the working of his mighty power, 20 Which he wrought in Christ, when he raised him from the dead, and set *him* at his own right hand

in the heavenly *places*,

__Sealed,__ pp. Furnished with a seal ; fastened with a seal ; confirmed ; closed.

__Seal,__ v.t. 8. To mark as one's own property, and secure from danger.

__Earnest,__ n. 2. First fruits ; that which is in advance, and gives promise of something to come.

Ephesians 4:30   And grieve not the holy Spirit of God, whereby ye are sealed unto the day of redemption.

2Corinthians 1:21,22   21 Now he which stablisheth us with you in Christ, and hath anointed us, *is* God; 22 Who hath also sealed us, and given the earnest of the Spirit in our hearts.

__Heart,__ n. [... , pulsation.] 1. A muscular viscus, which is the primary organ of the blood's motion in an animal body, situated in the thorax. From this organ all the arteries arise, and in it all the veins terminate. By its alternate dilatation and contraction, the blood is received from the veins, and returned through the arteries, by which means the circulation is carried on and life preserved.

2. The inner part of any thing; the middle part or interior; as the heart of a country, kingdom or empire ; as the heart of a town; the heart of a tree.

3. The chief part; the vital part; the vigorous or efficacious part.

4. The seat of the __affections__ and passions, as of love, joy, grief, enmity, courage, pleasure, &c.
The heart is deceitful above all things. Every imagination of the thought of the heart is evil continually. We read of an honest and good heart, and an evil heart of unbelief, a willing heart, a heavy heart, sorrow of heart, a hard heart, a proud heart, a pure heart. The heart faints in adversity, or under discouragement, that is, courage fails ; the heart is deceived, enlarged, reproved, lifted up, fixed, established, moved, &c. __Scripture.__

5. By a metonym, heart is used for an affection or passion, and particularly for love.
The king's heart was towards Absalom. **2Sam. xiv** .

__Affection,__ n.   3. A bent of mind toward a particular object, holding a middle place between disposition, which is natural, and passion, which is excited by the presence of its exciting object. Affection is a permanent bent of the mind, formed by the presence of an object, or by some act of another person, and existing without the presence of its object.

4. In a more particular sense, a __settled__ good will, love or zealous attachment.

__Settled,__ pp. Placed ; established ; fixed ; determined ; composed ; adjusted.

My personal notes:

He unifies us

1Corinthians 12:3

Wherefore I give you to understand, that no man speaking by the Spirit of God calleth Jesus accursed: and *that* no man can say that Jesus is the Lord, but by the Holy Ghost.

1Corinthians 12:12,13

12 For as the body is one, and hath many members, and all the members of that one body, being many, are one body: so also *is* Christ. 13 For **by one Spirit** are we all baptized into one body, whether *we be* Jews or Gentiles, whether *we be* bond or free; and have been all made to drink into one Spirit.

Drink, *v.t. 1. to receive 2. to absorb* → *To drink in, to absorb; to take or receive into any inlet.*

> ***My note:*** "so also is Christ." "For by one Spirit" "are we all baptized" "into" "one body,"

> ***My note:*** *We are baptized "***by*** one Spirit" ; this is spiritual baptism*

> ***My note:***
> *All believers make up the body of Christ; the oneness of Christ; by the Spirit of God, which dwelleth in us.*
> ***My note:***
> **Baptized:** *is (signifies and declares) the moving of a believer from, death of self (carnal nature)* → *to, the newness of life in Christ (spiritual nature); by the power of the Holy Spirit ; all to the glory of God the Father: by **one Spirit** & into **one body**!*

We are all one in Christ!

Ephesians 4:4 *There is* one body, and one Spirit, even as ye are called in one hope of your calling;

Ephesians 4:11 – 13 11 And he gave some, apostles; and some, prophets; and some, evangelists; and some,
Read: 4:1 – 24 pastors and teachers; 12 For the perfecting of the saints, for the work of the ministry, for the edifying of the body of Christ: 13 Till we all come in the unity of the faith, and of the knowledge of the Son of God, unto a perfect man, unto the measure of the stature of the fulness of Christ:

Read: **Galatians 3:26 – 28** 26 For ye are all the children of God by faith in Christ Jesus.

Colossians 3:15 , 16 15 And let the peace of God rule in your hearts, to the which also ye are called in one body; and be ye thankful. 16 Let the word of Christ dwell in you richly in all wisdom; teaching and admonishing one another in psalms and hymns and spiritual songs, singing with grace in your hearts to the Lord.

Romans 12:4, 5 4 For as we have many members in one body, and all members have not the same office: 5 So we, *being* many, are one body in Christ, and every one members one of another.

Into, *prep. 6. Noting the passing of a thing from one form or state to another.* *We are led by evidence into belief of truth.*

> ***My note:*** *The passing from* → *being carnal (carnally minded)* → *to* → *being spiritual (spiritually minded)*

Romans 8:5,6 5 For they that are after the flesh do mind the things of the flesh; but they that are after the Spirit
Read: Romans 8:1 - 17 the things of the Spirit. 6 For to be carnally minded *is* death; but to be spiritually minded *is* life and peace.

2Corinthians 5:17 Therefore if any man *be* in Christ, *he is* a new creature: old things are passed away; behold, all things are become new.

1John 4:13 Hereby know we that we dwell in him, and he in us, because he hath given us of his Spirit.

2Corinthians 5:5 Now he that hath wrought us for the selfsame thing *is* God, who also hath given unto us the earnest of the Spirit.

> ***My note:***
> Baptism is defined as the act of sprinkling or immersion into water. However, it declares as truth,
> ## Christ's own death, burial and resurrection; which gives a child of God eternal life!

1Corinthians 15:44 It is sown a natural body; it is raise a spiritual body. There is a natural body, and there is a spiritual body.

My personal notes:

Blessing with being filled with the Holy Ghost
He unifies us
continued...

baptism, signifies and declares
our own death & burial of self,

(It is a choice and a confession of an individual person. I am a sinner who is deserving of eternal separation from God and
I am deserving of eternal torment ; going to hell and then, to be cast into the lake of fire and brimstone, for ever ;
a just punishment for me being a sinner and for me rejecting Jesus Christ as the Son of God ; the Saviour of the world !)

Colossians 2:13
And you, being dead in your sins and in the uncircumcision of your flesh,
hath he quickened together with him, having forgiven you all trespasses;

Colossians 3:3
For ye are dead, and your life is hid with Christ in God.

Romans 8:8 – 10
10 And if Christ be in you, the body *is* dead because of sin; but the Spirit *is* life because of righteousness.

*(Accepting what Jesus Christ has done on the cross "*It is finished:*", taking upon himself the sins of the whole world and*
the eternal penalty for sin! paying my sin debt in full! So, my body is dead because of sin! and it is buried !)

2Corinthians 5:21
For he hath made him *to be* sin for us, who knew no sin; that we might be made the righteousness of God in him.

John 3:16
For God so loved the world, that he gave his only begotten Son, that whosoever believeth in him
should not perish, but have everlasting life.

John 1:29
The next day John seeth Jesus coming unto him, and saith, Behold the Lamb of God, which taketh away the sin of the world.

1John 2:2
And he is the propitiation for our sins: and not for ours only, but also for *the sins of* the whole world.

2Corinthians 5:19
To wit, that God was in Christ, reconciling the world unto himself, not imputing their trespasses unto them;
and hath committed unto us the word of reconciliation.

1John 4:14
And we have seen and do testify that the Father sent the Son *to be* the Saviour of the world.

Romans 6:3 – 14
4 Therefore we are buried with him by baptism into death: that like as Christ was raised up from the dead
by the gory of the Father, even so we also should walk in newness of life.

also:
Baptism, signifies and declares
our own resurrection to the newness of life, in Christ Jesus;
by the power of the Holy Ghost.

My note: I am alive in my Lord & my Saviour Jesus Christ; unto eternal life with HIM ! Even so, come, Lord Jesus. Revelation 22:20 … A-men'.

Romans 8:11
But if the Spirit of him that raised up Jesus from the dead dwell in you, he that raised up Christ from the dead
shall also quicken your mortal bodies by his Spirit that dwelleth in you.

Ephesians 2:4 – 10
4 But God, who is rich in mercy, for his great love wherewith he loved us, 5 Even when we were dead in sins,
hath quickened us together with Christ, (by grace ye are saved;) 6 And hath raised *us* up together,
and made *us* to sit together in heavenly *places* in Christ Jesus: 7 That in the ages to come he might shew
the exceeding riches of his grace in *his* kindness toward us through Christ Jesus.
8 For by grace are ye saved through faith; and that not of yourselves: *it is* the gift of God:
9 Not of works, lest any man should boast.

Romans 6:14
For sin shall not have dominion over you: for ye are not under the law, but under grace.

Read: **John 6:40 ; 10:28 (27-30) ; 11:14, 23 - 27 ; Acts 11:15 – 18 ; Romans 6:3 ;7:6 ; Galatians 6:8 ; 1Peter 2:2**

All to the glory of God the Father

Revelation 4:1 – 5:14

5:14 And the four beasts said, A-men'. And the four *and* twenty elders fell down and worshipped him that liveth for ever and ever.

Luke 2:13,14

13 And suddenly there was with the angel a multitude of heavenly host praising God, and saying,
14 Glory to God in the highest, and on earth peace, good will toward men.

My note: The only reference to Father in the Old Testament, where Father is capitalized as a proper noun, is **Isaiah 9:6** .
My note: Jesus Christ; the fulness of God Almighty! "God was manifest in the flesh" **1Timothy 3:16**

Isaiah 9:6 For unto us a child is born, unto us a son is given: and the government shall be upon his shoulder:
and his name shall be called Wonderful, Counsellor, The mighty God, The everlasting Father, The Prince of Peace.

My note:
The first reference to God as Father *; Father, as a proper noun.*

John 1:14

And the Word was made flesh, and dwelt among us, (and we beheld his glory, the glory as of
the only begotten of the Father,) full of grace and truth.

Also: **Matthew 5:16** ; **Mark 8:38**
and **Luke 6:36** ; **John 1:18; 3:35,36**

the last reference to God as Father *; Father, as a proper noun.*

Revelation 14:1

And I looked, and, lo, a Lamb stood on the mount Sion, and with him an hundred forty *and* four thousand,
having his Father's name written in their foreheads.

Revelation 3:21 To him that overcometh will I grant to sit with me in my throne, even as I also overcame, and am set down with my Father in his throne. 22 He that hath an ear, let him hear what the Spirit saith unto the churches.

Ephesians 1:17 That the God of our Lord Jesus Christ, the Father of glory, may give unto you the spirit of wisdom and revelation in the knowledge of him:

Philippians 2:10,11 10 That at the name of Jesus every knee should bow, of *things* in heaven, and *things* in earth, and *things* under the earth; 11 And *that* every tongue should confess that Jesus Christ *is* Lord, to the glory of God the Father.

Philippians 4:20 Now unto God and our Father *be* glory for ever and ever. A-men'.

My note: God is only the Father to those who are in the Lord Jesus Christ: born of the Spirit, unto the newness of life in God, our Father. We are heirs of God and joint-heirs with Jesus Christ, because we are children of the living God.

Matthew 6:8 – 13 8 Be not ye therefore like unto them: for your Father knoweth what things ye have need of, before ye ask him. 9 After this manner therefore pray ye: Our Father which art in heaven, Hallowed be thy name. 10 Thy kingdom come. Thy will be done in earth, as *it is* in heaven. 11 Give us this day our daily bread. 12 And forgive us our debts, as we forgive our debtors. 13 And lead us not into temptation, but deliver us from evil: For thine is the kingdom, and the power, and the glory, for ever. A-men'.

John 5:20, 21 20 For the Father loveth the Son, and sheweth him all things that himself doeth: and he will shew him
Read: 5:19 - 47 greater works than these, that ye may marvel. 21 For as the Father raiseth up the dead, and quickeneth *them*; even so the Son quickeneth whom he will.

John 14:9,10 9 Jesus saith unto him, Have I been so long time with you, and yet hast thou not known me, Philip? he that hath seen me hath seen the Father; and how sayest thou *then*, Shew us the Father? 10 Believest thou not that I am in the Father, and the Father in me? the words that I speak unto you I speak not of myself: but the Father that dwelleth in me, he doeth the works.

1Peter 5:10,11 10 But the God of all grace, who hath called us unto his eternal glory by Christ Jesus, after that ye have suffered a while, make you perfect, stablish, strengthen, settle *you*. 11 To him *be* glory and dominion for ever and ever. A-men'.

2Peter 1:17 For he received from God the Father honour and glory, when there came such a voice to him
from the excellent glory. This is my beloved Son, in whom I am well pleased.

John 8:3 And the scribes and Pharisees ...   *My note:* **John 8:19** "they" *refers to* "the scribes and Pharisees" **John 8:3**
John 8:19 Then said they unto him, Where is thy Father? Jesus answered, Ye neither know me, nor my Father:
if ye had known me, ye should have known my Father also.

John 17:5 And now, O Father, glorify thou me with thine own self with the glory which I had with thee before the world was.

He unifies us
continued...
baptism signifies and declares
continued...

1Corinthians 12:3
Wherefore I give you to understand, that no man speaking by the Spirit of God calleth Jesus accursed: and *that* no man can say that Jesus is the Lord, but by the Holy Ghost.

1Corinthians 12:12,13
12 For as the body is one, and hath many members, and all the members of that one body, being many, are one body: so also *is* Christ. 13 For **by one Spirit** are we all baptized into one body, whether *we be* Jews or Gentiles, whether *we be* bond or free; and have been all made to drink into one Spirit.

My note: Baptized also signifies (a sign of / makes known / declares) passing from **death** → *to* **life**.

FROM: the body of **death**   TO: the body of **life**, *eternal life with Jesus Christ*
                        V   V

carnal   **Jesus Christ is**   spiritual
outside   **the door**   inside
lost   John 10:7,9,10,11,14,28,29,30   saved
a child of wrath   *ETERNAL LIFE*   a child of God

My note:
Jesus Christ is the Door and HE is the Good Shepherd

John 10:7,8,9
7 Then said Jesus unto them again, Verily, verily, I say unto you, I am the door of the sheep.
8 All that ever came before me are thieves and robbers: but the sheep did not hear them.
9 I am the door: by me if any man enter in, he shall be saved, and shall go in and out, and find pasture.

John 10:11
I am the good shepherd: the good shepherd giveth his life for the sheep.

John 10:16
And other sheep I have, which are not of this fold: them also I must bring, and they shall hear my voice; and there shall be one fold, *and* one shepherd.

My note:
We (Gentiles) are the other sheep

John 10:28
And I give unto them eternal life; and they shall never perish, neither shall any *man* pluck them out of my hand.

Psalm 80:1 Give ear, O Shepherd of Israel, thou that leadest Joseph like a flock;
thou that dwellest *between* the cherubims, shine forth.

Matthew 26:31 Then saith Jesus unto them, All ye shall be offended because of me this night: for it is written, I will smite the shepherd, and the sheep of the flock shall be scattered abroad.

Hebrew 13:20,21 20 Now the God of peace, that brought again from the dead our Lord Jesus, that great shepherd of the sheep, through the blood of the everlasting covenant, 21 Make you perfect in every good work to do his will, working in you that which is wellpleasing in his sight, through Jesus Christ; to whom *be* glory for ever and ever. A-men'.
Read: **Mark 14:27; Hebrews 13:20; 1Peter 2:25; 5:4**

1Peter 5:4 And when the chief Shepherd shall appear, ye shall receive a crown of glory that fadeth not away.

1John 3:2 Beloved, now are we the sons of God, and it doth not yet appear what we shall be: but we know that, when he shall appear, we shall be like him; for we shall see him as he is.

My personal notes:

He unifies us

continued...

baptism, signifies and declares

continued...

1Corinthians 12:13

For <u>by one Spirit</u> are we all baptized into one body, ...; <u>and</u> ... made to drink <u>into one Spirit</u>.

<u>My note</u>:

We are baptized " <u>by one Spirit</u> " and " <u>into one Spirit</u> "

We " <u>have been all made to drink</u> " (receive)(absorb)

" <u>into</u> " (noting the passing of a thing from one form or state to another)

" <u>one Spirit</u> "

<u>Galatians 3:26</u> For ye are all the children of God by faith in Christ Jesus.

<u>Revelation 1:5</u>   And from <u>Jesus Christ</u>, ..., . Unto him that loved us, and <u>washed us from our sins in his own blood,</u>

<u>Titus 3:4 – 7</u> 4 But after that the kindness and love of God our Saviour toward man appeared, 5 Not by works of righteousness which we have done, but according to his mercy he saved us, by the <u>washing of regeneration,</u> and <u>renewing of the Holy Ghost;</u> 6 Which he shed on us abundantly through Jesus Christ our Saviour; 7 That being justified by his grace, we should be made heirs according to the hope of eternal life.

"washing of <u>regeneration</u>," *<u>My note</u>: What Noah's flood did physically, baptism does spiritually.*

See: Page 72 additional references Pages 1 & 2 .

<u>*Regeneration*</u>, *n.* *2. In theology, new birth by the grace of God; that change by which the will and natural enmity of man to God and his law are subdued, and a principle of supreme love of God and his law, or holy affections, are implanted in the heart.* **Tit. iii** .

<u>My note</u>: Baptism is a picture of (acknowledges) Christ's own death, burial and resurrection; which gives us eternal life with him.

<u>Luke 12:50</u> But <u>I have a baptism to be baptized with; and how am I straitened till it be accomplished!</u>

<u>Romans 6:3</u> Know ye not, that so many of us as were baptized into Jesus Christ were baptized into his death?
Read: 6:1 – 11

<u>Romans 6:8</u>   Now if we be dead with Christ, <u>we believe that we shall also live with him:</u>

<u>My note</u>: *Baptism acknowledges our own death (to self) and our own burial (of self) and our own resurrection (to the newness of life <u>in Christ</u> !)*

<u>Colossians 2:12 – 15</u> 12 <u>Buried with him in baptism,</u> wherein also ye are risen with *him* through the faith of the operation of God, who hath raised him from the dead. 13 And you, being dead in your sins and the uncircumcision of your flesh, hath he quickened together with him, having forgiven you all trespasses; 14 Blotting out the handwriting of ordinances that was against us, which was contrary to us, and took it out of the way, <u>nailing it to his cross;</u> 15 *And* having spoiled principalities and powers, he made a shew of them openly, triumphing over them in it.

<u>Colossians 3:1 – 4</u> 1 If ye then be risen with Christ, seek those things which are above, where Christ sitteth on the right hand of God. 2 Set your affection on things above, not on things on the earth. 3 <u>For ye are dead</u>, and <u>your life is hid with Christ in God</u>. 4 When Christ, *who is* our life, shall appear, then shall ye also appear with him in glory.

<u>1Peter 3:19</u>   ... the spirits in prison;

<u>1Peter 3:20</u>   Which sometime were disobedient, when once the longsuffering of God waited in the days of <u>Noah,</u> while the ark was a preparing, wherein few, that is, eight souls were <u>saved</u> <u>by water.</u>

<u>My note</u>: This saving " <u>by water</u>." was <u>by faith</u> – believing God's word as truth; Noah entered into the ark <u>by faith</u>; Noah was " <u>saved by water</u>."

<u>My note</u>: God compelled Noah, and his family, to enter into the ark and they did so, as the LORD commanded him.
        Genesis 7:16 ... , <u>as God commanded him</u>: <u>and the LORD shut him in</u>. *<u>My note</u>: Sealing them in the ark.*

<u>Genesis 7:12 – 16</u> 12 And the rain was upon the earth forty days and forty nights. 13 <u>In the selfsame day entered Noah, and Shem, and Ham, and Japheth, the sons of Noah, and Noah's wife, and the three wives of his sons with them, into the ark;</u> 14 They, and every beast after his kind, and all the cattle after their kind, and every creeping thing that creepeth upon the earth after his kind, and every fowl after his kind, every bird of every sort. 15 And they went in unto Noah into the ark, two and two of all flesh, wherein *is* the breath of life. 16 And <u>they</u> that <u>went in,</u> went in male and female of all flesh, <u>as God had commanded him</u>: <u>and the LORD shut him in</u>.

Romans 6:9 – 14   9 Knowing that Christ being raised from the dead dieth no more; death hath no more dominion over him. 10 For in that he died, he died unto sin once: but in that he liveth, he liveth unto God. 11 Likewise reckon ye also yourselves to be dead indeed unto sin, but alive unto God through Jesus Christ our Lord. 12 Let not sin therefore reign in your mortal body, that ye should obey it in the lusts thereof. 13 Neither yield ye your members *as* instruments of unrighteousness unto sin: but yield yourselves unto God, as those that are alive from the dead, and your members *as* instruments of righteousness unto God.

14 For sin shall not have dominion over you: for ye are not under the law, but under grace.

My personal notes:

He unifies us
continued…
baptism, signifies and declares
Additional References
Page 1

1Corinthians 12:13
For by one Spirit are we all baptized into one body, …; and … made to drink into one Spirit.

Titus 3:5 "washing of regeneration,"   *My note: What Noah's flood did physically, baptism does spiritually.*

My note: Saving those who believe and destroying those who do not believe ; those who have not repented.

1Peter 3:21 **15** But sanctify the Lord God in your hearts: and *be* ready always to *give* an answer to every man that asketh you a reason of the hope that is in you with meekness and fear: **16** Having a good conscience; that, whereas they speak evil of you, as of evildoers, they may be ashamed that falsely accuse your good conversation in Christ. **17** For *it is* better, if the will of God be so, that ye suffer for well doing, than for evil doing. **18** For Christ also once suffered for sins, the just for the unjust, that he might bring us to God, being put to death in the flesh, but quickened by the Spirit: **19** By which also he went and preached unto the spirits in prison; **20** Which sometime were disobedient, when once the longsuffering of God waited in the days of Noah, while the ark was a preparing, wherein few, that is, eight souls were saved by water. **21** The like figure whereunto *even* baptism doth also now save us (not the putting away of the filth of the flesh, but the answer of a good conscience toward God,) by the resurrection of Jesus Christ: **22** Who is gone into heaven, and is on the right hand of God; angels and authorities and powers being made subject
unto him.

Read: **Jude 1 – 25**   *vs.* **5** I will therefore put you in remembrance, though ye once knew this, how that the Lord, having saved the people out of the land of Egypt, afterward destroyed them that believed not.

Acts 2:38 Then Peter said unto them, Repent, and be baptized every one of you in the name of Jesus Christ
for the remission of sins, and ye shall receive the gift of the Holy Ghost.

Acts 8:12 But when they believed Philip preaching the things concerning the kingdom of God,
and the name of Jesus Christ, they were baptized, both men and women.

Acts 1:5 For John truly baptized with water; but ye shall be baptized with the Holy Ghost not many days hence.
Read: 1:1 - 14

Acts 11:16 Then remembered I the word of the Lord, how that he said, John indeed baptized with water;
Read: 1:1 - 18   but ye shall be baptized with the Holy Ghost.

Acts 19:3,4,5   **3** And he said unto them, Unto what then were ye baptized? And they said, Unto John's baptism.
Read: 19:1 - 7   **4** Then said Paul, John verily baptized with the baptism of repentance, saying unto the people, that they should believe on him which should come after him, that is, on Christ Jesus.
5 When they heard *this*, they were baptized in the name of the Lord Jesus.

Genesis 6:22 Thus did Noah; according to all that God commanded him, so did he.
Genesis 7:5 And Noah did according unto all that the LORD commanded him.

My note: Baptism is to willingly do what is commanded or declared of the LORD; Doing the will of God;
Submitting unto God the Father, the LORD.

My note: Noah believed God and he built the ark and he entered in, doing the will of the LORD; Noah was saved, physically and spiritually; from the flood and from the wrath of God to come. **Genesis 6:8,9; 7:23; 8:20,21,22; 9:1,8-17**

Hebrews 11:7 By faith Noah, being warned of God of things not seen as yet, moved with fear, prepared an ark to the saving of his house;
by the which he condemned the world, and became heir of the righteousness which is by faith.

Romans 6:3 – 14 **3** Know ye not, that so many of us as were baptized into Jesus Christ were baptized into his death?
My note: "baptized into Jesus Christ" *is to believe on him and to walk in HIS way; to do the will of God.*

Galatians 3:25 – 27 **25** But after that faith is come, we are no longer under a schoolmaster. **26** For ye are all the children of God by faith in Christ Jesus. **27** For as many of you as have been baptized into Christ have put on Christ.
My note: " put on " *is to believe on HIM and receive HIM , unto salvation.*

He unifies us
continued...
baptism, signifies and declares
Additional References
Page 2

1Corinthians 12:13

For by one Spirit are we all baptized into one body, ...; and ... made to drink into one Spirit.

Colossians 2:12 Buried with him in baptism, wherein also ye are risen with *him* through the faith of the operation of God, who hath raised him from the dead.

My note: " the operation of God " = " raised him from the dead. "

Acts 18:8 And Crispus, the chief ruler of the synagogue, believed on the Lord with all his house; and many of the Corinthians hearing believed, and were baptized.

Ephesians 4:5 **4** *There is* only one body, and one Spirit, even as ye are called in one hope of your calling; **5** One Lord, one faith, one baptism, **6** One God and Father of all, who *is* above all, and through all, and in you all.

My not: "one baptism " = *believing on the name of the Lord Jesus Christ unto salvation.*

Matthew 20:20 – 28 **22** But Jesus answered and said, **Ye know not what ye ask. Are ye able to drink of the cup that I shall drink of, and to be baptized with the baptism that I am baptized with?** They say unto him, We are able. **23** And he saith unto them, **Ye shall drink indeed of my cup, and be baptized with the baptism that I am baptized with: but to sit on my right hand, and on my left, is not mine to give, but *it shall be given to them* for whom it is prepared of my Father.**

Mark 10:35 – 45 **38** But Jesus said unto them, **Ye know not what ye ask: can ye drink of the cup that I drink of ? and be baptized with the baptism that I am baptized with?** **39** And they said unto him, We can. And Jesus said unto them, **Ye shall indeed drink of the cup that I drink of; and with the baptism that I am baptized withal shall ye be baptized:**

My note: verses **38 & 39** *declare: to believe God and to do HIS will.*

Luke 12:50 **But I have a baptism to be baptized with; and how am I straitened till it be accomplished!**

My note: " straitened " is to be overwhelmed or pressed to do what is necessary ; to do what must be done!
My note: Jesus was overwhelmed or pressed by HIS Father to accomplish what could only be done by HIM (Jesus Christ)!!!
My note: Words of Jesus: **" My soul is exceeding sorrowful, "** ; **" remove this cup from me: "** ; **" It is finished: "**

Matthew 26:36 – 44 **38** Then saith he unto them, My soul is exceeding sorrowful, **even unto death: tarry ye here, and watch with me.** **39** And he went a little farther, and fell on his face, and prayed, saying, **O my Father, if it be possible, let this cup pass from me: nevertheless not as I will, but as thou *wilt*.**

Mark 14:32 – 39 **35** And he went forward a little, and fell on the ground, and prayed that, if it were possible, the hour might pass from him. **36** And he said, **Abba, Father, all things *are* possible unto thee; take away this cup from me: nevertheless not what I will, but what thou wilt.**

Luke 22:41 – 44 **41** And he was withdrawn from them about a stone's cast, and kneeled down, and prayed, **42** Saying, **Father, if thou be willing, remove this cup from me: nevertheless not my will, but thine, be done.** **43** And there appeared an angel unto him from heaven, strengthening him. **44** And being in an agony he prayed more earnestly: and his sweat was as it were great drops of blood falling down to the ground.

John 17:4 **I have glorified thee on the earth: I have finished the work which thou gavest me to do.**
Read: 17:1 - 26

John 19:30 When Jesus therefore had received the vinegar, he said, **It is finished:** and he bowed his head, and gave up the ghost.

Strait, *n. A narrow pass or passage, ...* **2.** *Distress; difficulty; distressing necessity;*
Strait, *v.t. to put to difficulties.*
Straiten, *v.t.* **4.** *To distress; to perplex; to press with poverty or other necessity.*

He unifies us

continued...

baptism, signifies and declares

continued...

1Corinthians 12:3
Wherefore I give you to understand, that no man speaking by the Spirit of God calleth Jesus accursed: and *that* no man can say that Jesus is the Lord, but by the Holy Ghost.

1Corinthians 12:12,13
12 For as the body is one, and hath many members, and all the members of that one body, being many, are one body: so also *is* Christ. 13 For **by one Spirit** are we all baptized into one body, whether *we be* Jews or Gentiles, whether *we be* bond or free; and have been all made to drink into one Spirit.

1Peter 3:18,19   18 For Christ also hath once suffered for sins, the just for the unjust, that he might bring us to God, being put to death in the flesh, but quickened by the Spirit: 19 By which also he went and preached unto the spirits in prison;

1Peter 3:20 Which sometime were disobedient, when once the longsuffering of God waited in the days of Noah, while the ark was a preparing, wherein few, that is, eight souls were saved by water.

Figure, n. 12. In theology, type; representative.

Type, n.   2. A sign; a symbol; a figure of something to come;

My note: Type – a sign or symbol of something to come

My note: That which is to come is JUDGEMENT / GOD'S WRATH!

My note: All of the children of God are saved from the WRATH OF THE LAMB!

My note: " The like figure " is of vs. 20

1Peter 3:21 The like figure whereunto *even* baptism doth also now save us (not the putting away of the filth of the flesh, but the answer of a good conscience toward God,) by the resurrection of Jesus Christ:

My note: "(not the putting away of the filth of the flesh," which is the physical part of baptism, with the use of water to sprinkle, pour or submerge a person during the ceremony of baptism ; but baptism is "the answer of a good conscience toward God,)" ; the sincere acceptance of what Jesus Christ has done to save sinners. It is what Christ has done!!! So that, all who are HIS do not receive the WRATH OF GOD! THE WRATH OF THE LAMB!

1Peter 3:22 Who is gone into heaven, and is on the right hand of God; angels and authorities and powers being made subject unto him.

Revelations 6:16,17 16 And said to the mountains and rocks, Fall on us, and hide us from the face of him that sitteth on the throne, and from the wrath of the Lamb: 17 For the great day of his wrath is come; and who shall be able to stand?

BAPTISM is the ANSWER of YES to GOD!

My note:

Accepting what God has done through the Lord Jesus Christ as true and complete.

All of this through the power and influence of the Holy Ghost.

The ANSWER of (YES) → Hebrews 10:39 But we are not of them who draw back unto perdition; but of them that believe to the saving of the soul.

My note: Declaring Christ's death, burial and resurrection ; as, absolute truth.

From: page 74   **1Corinthians 12:12,13**

Gentile , *n.* [... , nation, race *; applied to pagans.]*

> *In the scriptures, a pagan ; a worshipper of false gods ; any person not a Jew or a christian ; a heathen.*
> *The Hebrews included in the term* goim *or nations, all the tribes of men who had not received the true faith,*
> *and were not circumcised. The christians translated* goem *by the L.* gentes, *and imitated the Jews in giving*
> *the name* gentiles *to all nations who were not Jews nor christians.*

Jew , *n.* [*a contraction of Judas or Judah.*] *A Hebrew or Israelite.*

My personal notes:

He unifies us

continued...

baptism, signifies and declares

continued...

BAPTISM is the ANSWER of YES to GOD!

Additional References

Page 1

Hebrews 10:38 Now the just shall live by faith: but if *any man* draw back, my soul shall have no pleasure in him.

Hebrews 10:39 But we are not of them who draw back unto perdition;
but of them that believe to the saving of the soul.

Perdition, n. [... , to lose, to ruin. ...] 2. The utter lose of the soul or of final happiness in a future state ;
future misery or eternal death.

Hebrews 11:1,2 1 Now faith is the substance of things hoped for, the evidence of things not seen.
2 For by it the elders obtained a good report.

Hebrews 11:3 Through faith we understand that the worlds were framed by the word of God,
so that things which are seen were not made of things which do appear.

Hebrews 11:6 But without faith *it is* impossible to please *him*: for he that cometh to God must believe that he is,
and *that* he is a rewarder of them that diligently seek him.

Hebrews 11:7 By faith Noah, being warned of God of things not seen as yet, moved with fear,
prepared an ark to the saving of his house; by the which he condemned the world,
and became heir of the righteousness which is by faith.

My note: Baptism is "The like figure" ; **Figure** *– type ; Type – a symbol of something to come.*

My note: We are compelled (commanded) that the only way to be saved is being in Christ (the ark), (as Noah did); to accept
Jesus Christ as our own personal Saviour and as our LORD. When we enter into Christ (the ark), as Noah did, we are
sealed by the Lord and we are given the "holy Spirit of promise, "*, the KING's seal, as the guarantee that we are HIS!*
Now and For Ever !!!

Ephesians 1:13,14 13 In whom ye also *trusted*, after that ye heard the word of truth, the gospel of your salvation: in whom also
after that ye believed, ye were sealed with that holy Spirit of promise, 14 Which is the earnest of our
inheritance until the redemption of the purchased possession, unto the praise of his glory.

1Peter 3:21 *My note: Baptism, believing God's word as true, saves us by the resurrection of Jesus Christ!*

My note: Baptized by faith; believing the testimony of God as absolute truth; believing God's word as true!

My note: First we receive Christ as our own personal Lord and Saviour by faith, believing God's word as truth.
Then we receive the Holy Spirit in our heart, as the guarantee from God that we are HIS!
And we are sealed with "that holy Spirit of promise".

Romans 8:15,16 15 For ye have not received the spirit of bondage again to fear; but ye have receive the Spirit of adoption,
whereby we cry, Abba, Father. 16 The Spirit itself beareth witness with our spirit, that we are the children
of God: 17 And if children, then heirs; heirs of God, and joint-heirs with Christ; if so be that we suffer with
him, that we may be also glorified together.

John 1:33,34 33 And I knew him not: but he that sent me to baptize with water, the same said unto me, Upon whom thou shalt
see the Spirit descending, and remaining on him, the same is he which baptizeth with the Holy Ghost.
34 And I saw and bare record that this is the Son of God.

My note:
Christ in me and me in Christ; The Father in me and me in the Father;
The Holy Ghost in me and me in the Holy Ghost; God in me and me in God;
TRUE PEACE!

He unifies us
continued...
baptism, signifies and declares
continued...
BAPTISM is the ANSWER of YES to GOD!
Additional References
Page 2

Titus 3:5 - 7 **5** Not by works of righteousness which we have done, but according to his mercy he saved us, by the washing of regeneration, and <u>renewing of the Holy Ghost</u>; **6** Which he shed on us abundantly <u>through Jesus Christ our Saviour</u>; **7** That <u>being justified by his grace</u>, we should be <u>made heirs according to the hope of eternal life</u>.

2Corinthians 5:17 Therefore if any man *be* in Christ, *he is* a new creature: old things pass away;

behold, all things are become new.

Philippians 4:7 And the <u>peace</u> of God, which <u>passeth</u> all understanding, shall <u>keep</u> your hearts and minds <u>through</u> Christ Jesus.

My note:, where we have true communion with God the Father! Through His Son, Jesus Christ! Now and for ever. A-men'.

Peace, *n. [..., <u>to appease</u>, ... <u>signifying to press or to stop</u>.]* *7. Harmony ; concord ; a state of reconciliation*

between parties at variance.

My note: to stop what? to stop God's wrath ; through the Lord Jesus Christ.

Pass, v.i. **19.** *To go beyond bounds.*
Passeth – *to go beyond bounds ;*   ***My note:*** *Not connected to this world's understanding.*

Keep *v.t.* **4.** *To preserve from falling or from danger; to protect; to guard or sustain.*
Keep, *v.t.* **20.** *To hold in one's own bosom*
          My note: *very intimate; as a loving Father keeps His child, in communion with Him! protecting HIS child!*

My note: *MY GOD KEEPS ME, THROUGH MY LORD AND SAVIOUR JESUS CHRIST, BY THE POWER OF THE HOLY GHOST*
          AND ALL TO THE GLORY OF GOD THE FATHER; NOW AND FOR EVER! A-MEN'.

Through, *prep.* **4.** *By means of ; by the agency of ; noting instrumentality.* Sanctify them through thy truth. **John xvii** .
          The gift of God is eternal life through Jesus Christ our Lord. **Rom. vi** .

John 17:17
Sanctify them through thy truth: <u>thy word is truth.</u>

Jesus (JESUS)	**Christ** (SAVIOUR)	**Jesus the Christ**	**Jesus** the <u>SAVIOUR</u>
His humanity	He is the Christ	Jesus THE ANOINTED ONE	God manifest in the flesh **1Timothy 3:16**
He is Jesus	He is THE ANOINTED ONE	***Christ***, *n. THE ANOINTED*	**John 1:1 - 14**

Read:

John 1:12 ; 6;40 ; 11:25 – 27 ; 20:31 ; Acts 8:37*(vs. 26-30&31-35&36-38&39,40)* **; 16:31***(vs. 30-34)* **; 1John 5:10 – 13**

Blessing with being filled with the Holy Ghost
He unifies us
continued...

1Peter 3:21 The like figure whereunto *even* baptism doth also now save us (not the putting away of the filth of the flesh, but the answer of a good conscience toward God,) by the resurrection of Jesus Christ:

My note: *Baptism, if sincere, is the answer (yes) of a good conscience to God.*

John 10:14 – 18 14 I am the good shepherd, and know my *sheep,* and am known of mine. 15 As the Father knoweth me, even so know I the Father: and I lay down my life for the sheep. 16 And other sheep I have, which are not of this fold: them also I must bring, and they shall hear my voice; and there shall be one fold, *and* one shepherd. 17 Therefore doth my Father love me, because I lay down my life, that I might take it again. 18 No man taketh it from me, but I lay it down of myself. I have power to lay it down, and I have power to take it again. This commandment have I received of my Father.

My note: *Jesus Christ had "*a baptism to be baptized with;*"* **Luke 12:50** *THE CROSS*

My note: *"THE CROSS"; Jesus saying, Yes to HIS Father, and HIM paying the sin debt in full!!!*

My note:
Christ's own obedience unto his own death **Matthew** 27:**50** ; **Mark** 10:33,**34** ; 15:**37** ; **Luke** 18:**33** ; 23:**46** ; **John** 19:**30**,**33**

John 19:30 When Jesus therefore had received the vinegar, he said, It is finished: and he bowed his head, and gave up the ghost.

Christ's own obedience unto his own burial **Matthew** 26:**12** ; 27:57 - **60**; **Mark** 15:43 - 46,**47**; **Luke** 23:50 - **55**; **John** 19:38 - 42

Christ's own obedience unto his own resurrection, the newness of life **Matthew** 28:1 - 4,5, **6** ; **Mark** 10:**34** ;16:1 – **6** , **9**-20
Luke 18:**33** ; 24:1,**2** , **3** - 6, **7** , 21 – 26 ; 46 ; 50 - 53
John 20:1, **2** – 8, **9** ,10 - 16, **17** ,18 - 31

My note:
To be filled with the Spirit is to focus on Jesus Christ
and
His redemptive work upon the cross at Calvary!
Christ is every thing
and
I am nothing, without HIM!

Ephesians 5:18 – 20

18 And be not drunk with wine, wherein is excess; but be filled with the Spirit; 19 Speaking to yourselves in psalms and hymns and spiritual songs, singing and making melody in your heart to the Lord; 20 Giving thanks always for all things unto God and the Father in the name of our Lord Jesus Christ; 21 Submitting yourselves one to another in the fear of God.

John 15:5
I am the vine, ye *are* the branches: He that abideth in me, and I in him, the same bringeth forth much fruit:
for without me ye can do nothing.

John 3:36
He that believeth on the Son hath everlasting life:
and he that believeth not the Son shall not see life; but the wrath of God abideth on him.

My note: *The Holy Ghost and Jesus Christ and God the Father , dwell in every born again believer!*
My note: *Almighty God, dwells in every one who is born again! Declaring who is HIS! now and for ever!!!*

John 14:6,7,9,10,11,16,17,18,20,21,23,26

My personal notes:

The Cross

the atoning sacrifice

/\

1John 2:2

And he is the <u>propitiation</u> for our sins: and not for ours only, but for *the sins of* the whole world.

Propitious, a. **2.** *Disposed to be gracious or merciful;* <u>*ready to forgive sins and bestow blessings;*</u> *applied to God.*

<u>Reconciling</u>

/\

Propitiation, *n.* **1.** *The act of appeasing wrath and* <u>*conciliating*</u> *the favor of an offended person; the act of making* <u>*propitious*.</u>
2. *In theology, the* <u>*atonement*</u> *or* <u>*atoning sacrifice*</u> *offered to God to assuage his wrath and render him*
<u>*propitious*</u> *to sinners.* *Christ is the propitiation for the sins of men.* **Rom. iii . 1John ii .**

Conciliate, *v.t.* [*..., to draw or bring together, to unite; ...*] **2.** *To reconcile, or bring to a state of friendship, as persons at variance.*
Conciliating, *ppr. Winning; engaging;* <u>*reconciling*.</u>

Reconciling, *ppr.* <u>*Bringing into favor and friendship after variance;*</u> <u>*bring to content or satisfaction*</u>

Reconcile, *v.t.* [*... The literal sense is* <u>*to call back into union*.</u>] **1.** <u>*To call back into union and friendship*</u> *the affections which have*
<u>*been alienated;*</u> <u>*to restore to friendship or favor after*</u> *estrangement;*
Go thy way; first be reconciled to thy brother -- **Matt. v**
We pray you in Christ's stead, be ye reconciled to God. **2Cor. v . ; Eph. ii . ; Col. i .**

Estrangement, *n. Alienation; a keeping at a distance; removal;* **My note:** *a withdrawing of affections*

Atonement, *n.* **3.** *In theology, the* <u>*expiation*</u> *of sin made by the obedience and personal sufferings of Christ.*

Expiation, *n. The act of atoning for a crime;* <u>*the act of making satisfaction for an offense,*</u> *by which the guilt is done away,*
<u>*and the obligation of the offended person to punish the crime is canceled;*</u> *atonement;* <u>*satisfaction.*</u>

My note: *The crime is Adam rejecting God's word as truth. The crime is Adam eating of the tree of the knowledge of good and evil and Adam*
not believing God ; <u>*Adam not holding fast to God's word as absolute truth.*</u>
My note: *The penalty for sin (the crime) is death.* **Rom. 5:14 ; 1Cor. 15:22** *Read:* **Genesis 2:15,16,17 *and* 3:1 - 24**

ATONING SACRIFICE

Atoning, *ppr.* <u>*Reconciling.*</u> *Obs.* **2.** <u>*Making amends, or satisfaction.*</u> *Read:* **Romans 5:1 - 21**

Sacrifice, *n. The thing offered to God, or immolated by an act of religion.* **My note:** *Jesus Christ, upon the cross at Calvary;*

My note: *HIS rejection and HIS physical suffering and HIS physical death and HIS descending into hell; HIS separation from God, HIS Father!*

Matthew 27:46 ... Jesus cried ... , <u>My God, my God, why hast thou forsaken me?</u>

Mark 15:34 ... Jesus cried ... , <u>My God, my God, why hast thou forsaken me?</u>

2Corinthians 5:21 For he hath made him *to be* sin for us, who knew no sin;
Read: 5:14 - 21 that we might be made the righteousness of God in him.

Hebrews 2:17 Wherefore in all things it behoved him to be made like unto *his* brethren, that he might be a merciful
and faithful high priest in things *pertaining* to God, to make <u>reconciliation</u> for the sins of the people.

Reconciliation, *n.* **2.** *In Scripture,* <u>*the means by which sinners are reconciled*</u> *and* <u>*brought into a state of favor*</u>
<u>*with God, after natural estrangement or enmity;*</u> *the atonement;* <u>*expiation.*</u>

John 1:29 The next day John seeth <u>Jesus</u> coming unto him, and saith, Behold <u>the Lamb of God,</u>
<u>which taketh away the sin of the world.</u>

Read: **1John 1:1 – 5:21**

1John 4:10 Herein is love, <u>not that we loved God,</u> <u>but that he loved us</u>, and sent his Son *to be* the <u>propitiation</u> for our sins.

1John 4:13 Hereby know we that we dwell in him, and he in us, because <u>he hath given us of his Spirit.</u>

1John 4:14 - 19 **14** And we have seen and do testify that the Father sent the Son *to be* the Saviour of the world. **15** <u>Whosoever</u>
<u>shall confess that Jesus is the Son of God,</u> <u>God dwelleth in him,</u> <u>and he in God.</u> **16** And we have known and
believed the love that God hath to us. God is love; and he that dwelleth in love dwelleth in God, and God in
him. **17** Herein is our love made perfect, <u>that we may have boldness in the day of judgment:</u> because as
he is, so are we in this world. **18** There is no fear in love; but perfect love casteth out fear: because fear hath
torment. He that feareth is not made perfect in love. **19** <u>We love him</u>, because <u>he first loved us.</u>

Eternity is outside of time.

Christ stepped into time, yet HE is eternal.	**1Timothy 3:16**	*HE was clothed in the flesh.*
Christ Jesus	**John1:14**	**Jesus Christ**
(*"as a man" ; flesh and blood ; the humanity of Christ*)	**Philippians 2:5 – 11**	(*" the form of a servant " ; " the likeness of men "*)
		(*"And being found in fashion as a man,"*)

1Timothy 2:5 For *there is* one God, and one mediator between God and men, <u>the man</u> Christ Jesus;

Hebrews 2:9 – 18 9 But we see <u>Jesus,</u> who <u>was made a little lower than the angels</u> for the suffering of death, crowned with glory and honour: <u>that he</u> by the grace of God <u>should taste death for every man</u>. **10** For it became him, for whom *are* all things, and by whom *are* all things, in bringing many sons unto glory, to make the captain of their salvation perfect through sufferings. **11** For both he that sanctifieth and they who are sanctified, *are* all of one: for which cause he is not ashamed to call them brethren, **12** Saying, I will declare thy name unto my brethren, in the midst of the church will I sing praise unto thee. **13** And again, I will put my trust in him. And again, Behold I and the children which God hath given me. **14** Forsomuch then <u>as the children are partakers of flesh and blood,</u> <u>he also himself likewise took part of the same;</u> that through death he might destroy him that had the power of death, that is, the devil; **15** And deliver them who through fear of death were all their lifetime subject to bondage. **16** For verily he took not on *him the nature* of angels; but <u>he took on *him* the seed of Abraham</u>. **17** Wherefore in all things it behoved him to be made like unto *his* brethren, that he might be a merciful and faithful high priest in things *pertaining* to God, to make reconciliation for the sins of the people. **18** <u>For in that</u> <u>he himself hath suffered being tempted,</u>
<u>he is able to succour them that are tempted.</u>

Romans 8:1 – 4 **1** *There is* therefore now no condemnation to them which are in <u>Christ Jesus,</u> who walk not after the flesh, but after the Spirit. **2** For the law of the Spirit of life in <u>Christ Jesus</u> hath made me free from the law of sin and death. **3** For what the law could not do, in that it was weak through the flesh, <u>God sending his own Son in the likeness of sinful flesh</u>, and for sin, <u>condemned sin in the flesh</u>: **4** That the righteousness of the law might be fulfilled in us, who walk not after the flesh, but after the Spirit.

My personal notes:

The Cross
continued...

<u>**Christ**</u>, *n.* [*... anointed, from ..., to anoint.*] <u>*THE ANOINTED*</u>; *an appellation given to the Savior of the world,*
and synonymous with the Hebrew <u>*MESSIAH*</u>

<u>**Messiah**</u>, *n.* [*Heb. ..., anointed.*] *Christ, the anointed; the Savior of the world*   I know that when <u>Messiah</u> cometh,
who is called <u>Christ</u>, he will tell us all things.
<u>Jesus</u> answered her, <u>I that speak to thee am he</u>. **John iv** .

<u>John 1:1</u>
In the beginning was the Word, and the Word was with God, and the Word was God.

Jesus Christ took upon himself, the sins of the whole world!!!

<u>2Corinthians 5:21</u>
For he hath made him *to be* sin for us, who knew no sin;
that we might be made the righteousness of God in him.

My note:

HE ENDURED AN ETERNITY'S WORTH OF GOD'S WRATH!!!

Jesus Christ endured the fulness of the wrath and separation of God, HIS Father, an eternity's worth,
in a very short period of time, <u>as we know time</u> ; an eternity's worth.

<u>AN ETERNITY'S WORTH IS ILLUSTRATED IN THIS WAY:</u>

A person takes upon himself the cut on the finger and the pain; for another person.

If you cut your own finger because of your own neglect and carelessness, it is your own fault; it hurts, but it is your own neglect and carelessness and your own fault, so you endure; It is a just penalty or consequence!

If a person takes upon himself, billions of cuts on the finger all at the same time, the intensity of the pain is multiplied and magnified! If a person endures the fullness of the pain over a short period of time, the pain is magnified and intensified because it is the fullness of all the pain, <u>which would have been stretched out over time</u>, <u>being received in a short amount of time</u> ; *an eternity's worth of the wrath and separation of God, HIS Father!*

This is a simple and incomplete illustration of some of what Jesus Christ endured for us and when considering what Jesus endured, keep in mind, HE was completely rejected by HIS Father because of the sin of the whole world;

the sin from Adam → and continuing on → my sin → → →

HE, "who knew no sin;" **2Corinthians 5:21**

<u>**Hebrews 12:2**</u>   Looking unto Jesus the author and finisher of *our* faith; who for the joy that was set before him endured the cross, despising the shame, and is set down at the right hand of the throne of God.

<u>**Romans 6:13**</u> Neither yield ye your members *as* instruments of unrighteousness unto sin: but yield yourselves unto God, as those that are alive from the dead, and your members *as* instruments of righteousness unto God. **14** For <u>sin shall not have</u> <u>dominion</u> <u>over you</u>: for <u>ye are not under the law</u>, <u>but under grace</u>.

<u>*Dominion*</u>, *n.* *2. Power to direct , control, use and dispose of at pleasure; right of possession and use without being accountable;*

<u>**My note:**</u> *Every act of righteousness continually affirms the LOVE and HOLINESS and RIGHTEOUSNESS of GOD because, true acts of righteousness are of Christ, by the power of the Holy Spirit and all to the glory of God the Father.*

<u>**Romans 6:22,23**</u> **22** But now being made free from sin, and become servants to God, ye have your fruit unto holiness, and the end everlasting life. **23** For the wages of sin *is* death; but the gift of God *is* eternal life through Jesus Christ our Lord.

The Cross

continued...

Romans 8:1-7 1 *There is* therefore now no condemnation to them which are in Christ Jesus, who walk not after the flesh, but after the Spirit. 2 For the law of the Spirit of life in Christ Jesus hath made me free from the law of sin and death. 3 For what the law could not do, in that it was weak through the flesh, God sending his own Son in the likeness of sinful flesh, and for sin, condemned sin in the flesh: 4 That the righteousness of the law might be fulfilled in us, who walk not after the flesh, but after the Spirit. 5 For they that are after the flesh do mind the things of the flesh; but they that are after the Spirit the things of the Spirit. 6 For to be carnally minded *is* death; but to be spiritually minded *is* life and peace.

Hebrews 3:1 Wherefore, holy brethren, partakers of the heavenly calling, consider the Apostle and High Priest of our profession, Christ Jesus;

Hebrews 4:14-16 14 Seeing then that we have a great high priest, that is passed into the heavens, Jesus the Son of God, let us hold fast *our* profession. 15 For we have not an high priest which cannot be touched with the feeling of our infirmities; but was in all points tempted like as *we are, yet* without sin. 16 Let us therefore come boldly unto the throne of grace, that we may obtain mercy, and find grace to help in time of need.

1Timothy 3:16 And without controversy great is the mystery of godliness: God was manifest in the flesh, justified in the Spirit, seen of angels, preached unto the Gentiles, believed on in the world, received up into glory.

Mystery, n. 2. *In religion, any thing in the character or attributes of God, or in the economy of divine providence, which is not revealed to man.* President Moore.

3. *That which is beyond human comprehension until explained.* In this sense, mystery often conveys the idea of something awfully *sublime* or important; something that excites wonder.

Great is the mystery of godliness. **1Tim. iii** . *vs. 16*
Having made known unto us the mystery of his will, **Eph. i** . *vs. 9*
We speak the wisdom of God in a mystery. **1Col. ii** . *vs. 7 - 13*

Sublime, a. *High in style or sentiment ; lofty ; grand* .
Grand, a. *Noble; sublime; lofty; conceived or expressed with great dignity*

Justified, pp. *My note: Proven or shown to be just, or conformed to law ; (God's law) ; Jesus was* " God manifest in the flesh,"
Justify, v.t. *[..., just, and ... to make.]* 1. *To prove or show to be just, or conformable to law, right, justice, propriety or duty;*
2. *In theology, to pardon and clear from guilt; to absolve or acquit from guilt and merited punishment, and to accept as righteous on account of the merits of the Savior, or by the application of Christ's atonement to the offender.*

John 10:7 - 11 7 Then said Jesus unto them again, Verily, verily, I say unto you, I am the door of the sheep. 8 All that ever came before me are thieves and robbers: but the sheep did not hear them. 9 I am the door: by me if any man enter in, he shall be saved, and shall go in and out, and find pasture. 10 The thief cometh not, but for to steal, and to kill, and to destroy: I am come that they might have life, and that they might have *it* more abundantly. 11 I am the good shepherd: **the good shepherd giveth his life for the sheep.**

Read:

Isaiah 52:14,15

and

become grounded in its truth, before moving on!

Jesus Christ

Isaiah 52:14,15

Visage, *n.* The face ; the countenance or look of a person

⋀   *Mar*, *v.t.* **4.** To injure; to deform; to disfigure.

14 As many were **astonied** at thee; his visage was so marred more than any man,

and his form more than the sons of men:

⋁

Form, *n.* **1.** The shape or external appearance
of the body

Purify, *v.t.* **3.** To free from guilt or the defilement of sin; **Tit. ii**

Sprinkle, *v.t.* **3.** To wash; to cleanse; to purify

Titus 2:14

15 So shall he sprinkle many nations; the kings shall shut their mouths at him:

for *that* which had not been told them shall they see;

and *that* which they had not heard shall they consider.

Astonied, *pp.* astonished

Astonish, *v.t.* [... The primary sense is, to stop, to strike dumb, to fix.] To stun or strike with sudden fear,
terror, surprise or wonder; to amaze ; to confound with some sudden passion.

I Daniel was astonished at the vision. **Dan. viii** .

Astonished, *pp.* Amazed ; confounded with fear, surprise, or admiration.

Amaze, *v.t.* [To perplex or confuse] To confound with fear, sudden surprise, or wonder; to astonish.
This word implies astonishment or perplexity, arising from something
extraordinary, unexpected, unaccountable, or frightful.

Amazed, *pp.* Astonished ; confounded with fear, surprise or wonder.

Confound, *v.t.* **6.** To perplex with terror; to terrify; to dismay; to astonish; to throw into consternation;
to stupify with amazement.

The multitude came together and were confounded. **Acts ii.** ; Acts 2:6

Confounded, *pp.* Mixed or blended in disorder; perplexed; abashed; dismayed; put to shame and silence;
astonished.

Dismay, *v.t.* [...The sense then is to deprive of strength. To faint.] To deprive of that strength or
firmness of mind which constitutes courage; hence, to affright or terrify.

Terrify, *v.t.* To frighten; to alarm or shock with fear.

Consternation, *n.* [.., to throw or strike down.] Astonishment; amazement or horror that confounds
the faculties, and incapacitates a person for
(to speak) consultation and execution (to do) ;
excessive terror, wonder or surprise. South.

Stupify, *v.t.*

Stupefy, *v.t.* **1.** To make stupid; to make dull, to blunt the faculty of perception or understanding;
to deprive of sensibility. **2.** To deprive of material motion.

Isaiah 53:1-12

1 Who hath believed our report? and to whom is the arm of the LORD revealed?

2 For he shall grow up before him as a tender plant, and as a root out of a dry ground:
he hath no form nor comeliness; and when we shall see him,
there is no beauty that we should desire him.

3 He is despised and rejected of men; a man of sorrows, and acquainted with grief:
and we hid as it were *our* faces from him; he was despised, and we esteemed him not.

4 Surely he hath borne our griefs, and carried our sorrows:
yet we did esteem him stricken, smitten of God; and afflicted.

5 But he *was* wounded for our transgressions, *he was* bruised for our iniquities:
the chastisement of our peace *was* upon him; and with his stripes we are healed.

6 All we like sheep have gone astray; we have turned every one to his own way;
and the LORD hath laid on him the iniquity of us all.

7 He was oppressed, and he was afflicted, yet he opened not his mouth:
he is brought as a lamb to the slaughter, and as a sheep before her shearers is dumb,
so he openeth not his mouth.

8 He was taken from prison and from judgment: and who shall declare his generation?
for he was cut off out of the land of the living:
for the transgression of my people was he stricken.

9 And he made his grave with the wicked, and with the rich in his death;
because he had done no violence, neither *was any* deceit in his mouth.

10 Yet it pleased the LORD to bruise him; he hath put *him* to grief:
when thou shalt make his soul an offering for sin, he shall see *his* seed,
he shall prolong *his* days, and the pleasure of the LORD shall prosper in his hand.

11 He shall see of the travail of his soul, *and* shall be satisfied: by his knowledge
shall my righteous servant justify many; for he shall bear their iniquities.

12 Therefore will I divide him *a portion* with the great, and he shall divide the spoil
with the strong; because he hath poured out his soul unto death:
and he was numbered with the transgressors;
and he bare the sin of many, and
made intercession for the transgressors.

Deuteronomy 21:22,23

22 And if a man have committed a sin worthy of death, and he be to be put to death,
and
thou hang him on a tree:

23 His body shall not remain all night upon the tree,
but
thou shalt in any wise bury him that day;

(for he that is hanged *is* accursed of God;)

that thy land be not defiled,

which the LORD thy God giveth thee

for an inheritance.

1John 2:1,2

1 My little children,
these things write I unto you, that ye sin not.
And if any man sin,
we have an advocate with the Father,

Jesus Christ the righteous:

2 And he is the propitiation for our sins:
and not for ours only,
but also for *the sins of* the whole world.

Advocate, n. [..., *to plead for;* ...] *1. Advocate, in its primary sense, signifies,*
one who pleads the cause of another in a court of civil law. Hence,
2. One who pleads the cause of another before any tribunal or judicial court,
3. One who defends, vindicates, or espouses a cause by argument; one who is friendly to;
as, an advocate for peace, or for the oppressed.
In scripture, Christ is called an advocate for his people.
We have an advocate *with the father.* **1John ii .**

Propitiation, n. *2. In theology, the atonement or atoning sacrifice offered to God to assuage his wrath and*
render him propitious *to sinners. Christ is the propitiation for the sins of men.* **Romans iii . 1John ii .**

Propitious, a. *2. Disposed to be gracious or merciful; ready to forgive sins and bestow blessings ; applied to God.*

My note: Jesus Christ took upon himself the sins of the whole world. **1John 2:2**

Deuteronomy 21:22,23

Accursed, pp. Doomed to destruction or misery; 3. Worthy of the curse; detestable; execrable.

Curse, n. 4. Condemnation; sentence of divine vengeance on sinners. **Gal. iii .**

Detestable, a. Extremely hateful ; abominable ; very odious ; deserving abhorrence. **Ezek. v. .**

Detest, v.t. [... To detest is to thrust away.] To abhor ; to abominate ; to hate extremely ;

Execrable, a. Deserving to be cursed ; very hateful ; detestable ; abominable ;

Romans 6:23 For the wages of sin *is* death; but the gift of God *is* eternal life through Jesus Christ our Lord.

My note:

What is the curse? *Death & hell ; the eternal wrath, separation and rejection of God, by God, from God the Father.*
My note: Loss of fellowship with the LORD! **Genesis 3:10** ... I was afraid, ...

Genesis 2:15 – 17   **Genesis 3:13 – 19**   **Genesis 3:23,24**
Genesis 2:17 ... thou shalt surely die.   **Genesis 3:24** So he drove out the man; ...

John 1:29	*RECINCILED*	**2Corinthians 5:19**	*RECINCILED*	**Hebrews 12:2**
"... , Behold	*IN CHRIST*	V	*IN CHRIST*	V
the Lamb of God,		"... , reconciling the world		"for the joy that was set before him"
***Christ*'s focus**		*Eternity*	*Eternity*	*Eternity*
which taketh away	*RECONCILED*	unto himself, ..."	*RECONCILED*	"endured the cross,"
the sin of the world."	*IN CHRIST*		*IN CHRIST*	"despising the shame,"
		Isaiah 53:11,12		

ACCURSED

2Corinthians 5:21 For he hath made him *to be* sin for us, who knew no sin; ...
John 1:29 ..., Behold the Lamb of God, which taketh away the sin of the world.
1Peter 2:24 Who his own self bare our sins in his own body on the tree, ...

My note:

One part of God's wrath is being pronounced (determined / declared) to receive,
another part of God's wrath is being rejected by God (the rejection of God and from God) ,
then receiving the actual wrath of God (by God and from Almighty God) .

Accursed

God	determining	Jesus Christ as worthy of the curse
the > > > >	declaring > > > > >	because he (Christ) took upon himself
Father	pronouncing	the sins of the whole world. **1John 2:2**

AND THEN JESUS CHRIST WAS REJECTED AND SEPARATED FROM GOD, HIS FATHER
AND THEN DEATH AND THEN JESUS DESCENDED INTO HELL!
HE PAID THE SIN DEBT IN FULL!

CROSS

ACCURSED OF GOD
Hebrews 12:2
"endured the cross,"

ACCURSED OF GOD	HANGED ON A TREE	AN ETERNITY OF THE SEPARATION OF GOD	DEATH AND HELL
God pronouncing **Christ** *as worthy of the cross because of taking upon* **HIMSELF** *the sins of the whole world* **1John 2:2**	**Deuteronomy 21:22, 23** **Galatians 3:12** **Acts 5:30** **Acts 10:39** **1Peter 2:24**	AN ETERNITY OF THE SEPARATION OF GOD	THE WRATH OF GOD
Jesus Christ suffered *AN ETERNITY'S WORTH*		**Romans 6:23** "For the wages of sin *is* death;"	

RECONCILED IN CHRIST	Colossians 1:20-22 2Corinthians 5:14 – 21 Hebrews 2:17 Romans 5:10	Revelation 3:21 Revelation 5:10 - 14 "Worthy is the Lamb"	*Eternal fellowship with his own*	1Corinthians 1:7-9 1John 1:3
Eternity	*Eternity*	*Eternity*		*Eternity*
1John 2:2	**John 1:29**	**Hebrews 12:2** "and is set down at the right hand of the throne of God."	*Eternal fellowship with his own*	**Revelation 1:5,6**
RECONCILED IN CHRIST	Revelation 21:1 – 22:21			

ACCURSED OF GOD
Hebrews 12:2
"despising the shame,"

Despise, v.t. 1. To contemn *; to scorn ; to disdain ;* to have the lowest opinion of*. 2. to* abhor*.*
Despising, *ppr.* Contemning ; scorning ; disdaining. Abhorred, *pp.* Hated extremely,

Contemn, v.t. 2. To slight ; to neglect as unworthy of regard ; to reject with disdain.
Contemning, ppr. Despising ; slighting as vile or despicable ; neglecting or rejecting, as unworthy of regard.

ACCURSED OF GOD	HANGED ON A TREE	AN ETERNITY OF THE SEPARATION OF GOD	DEATH AND HELL
God rejecting **Jesus Christ** *because of HIM taking upon* **HIMSELF** *the sins of the whole world* **1John 2:2**	*Forsaken by God* **Matthew 27:46** **Mark 15:34** **Psalm 22:1** *(fulfilled)*	AN ETERNITY OF THE SEPARATION OF GOD	THE WRATH OF GOD
Jesus Christ suffered *AN ETERNITY'S WORTH*	**Romans 6:23** "For the wages of sin *is* death;"		

<u>*My note:*</u> *The Lord Jesus Christ* hated "despising *the shame,"* *of being rejected by God, HIS Father!!!*
Isaiah 53:6,9 *(53:1-12)* ; **John 19:19** ; **2Corinthians 5:21**

He is risen
and
He has prepared a place for HIS own
the children of the one true God ;
HIS children, who are **worthy** *to walk in HIS way ;*
teaching and preaching the gospel of the Lord Jesus Christ !

Isaiah 9:6
"Wonderful, Councellor, The might God, The everlasting Father, The Prince of Peace."
John 1:29
"Lamb of God,"

Revelation 15:3 And they sing the song of Moses the servant of God, and the song of the Lamb, saying, Great and marvellous *are* thy works, Lord God Almighty; just and true *are* thy ways, thou King of saints.

Revelation 17:14 These shall make war with the Lamb, and the Lamb shall overcome them: for he is Lord of lords, and King of kings: and they that are with him *are* called, and chosen, and faithful.

Revelation 19:16 And he hath on *his* vesture and on his thigh a name written, KING OF KING, AND LORD OF LORDS.

Revelation 22:13
I am Alpha and Omega, the beginning and the end, the first and the last.
Revelation 22:16
I Jesus have sent mine angel to testify unto you these things in the churches. I am the root and the offspring of David, *and* the bright and morning star.

My note:
By the declaring of the Holy Ghost, consider yourself as an honored and worthy servant *of God,* to teach *and* to preach *the* Word *of God,* as the Spirit of God leads you*. In the name of* the Lord Jesus Christ, *by* the power of the Holy Spirit *and to* the glory of the Father.

HE is risen !

Matthew 28:1,2 **1** In the end of the sabbath, as it began to dawn toward the first *day* of the week, came Mary Magdalene and the other Mary to see the sepulchre. **2** And, behold, there was a great earthquake: for the angel of the Lord descended from heaven, and came and rolled back the stone from the door, and sat upon it.

Matthew 28:6 He is not here: for he is risen, as he said. Come, see the place where the Lord lay.

Matthew 28:9, 10 **9** And as they went to tell his disciples, behold, Jesus met them, saying, All hail. And they came and held him by the feet, and worshipped him. **10** Then said Jesus unto them, Be not afraid: go tell my brethren that they go into Galilee, and there shall they see me.

1Thessalonians 1:10 And to wait for his Son from heaven, whom he raised from the dead, *even* Jesus, which delivered us from the wrath to come.

Declared by the Lord Jesus Christ as being worthy of heaven !

Colossians 1:10 That ye might walk worthy of the Lord unto all pleasing, being fruitful in every good work,
Read: 1:1 - 29   and increasing in the knowledge of God;

Colossians 1:19 For it pleased *the Father* that in him should all fulness dwell;

Colossians 2:9 For in him dwelleth all the fulness of the Godhead bodily.

1Thessalonians 1:5 For our gospel came not unto you in word only, but also in power, and in the Holy Ghost, and in much assurance; as ye know what manner of men we were among you for your sake. **6** And ye became followers of us, and of the Lord, having received the word in much affliction, with joy of the Holy Ghost:

1Thessalonians 2:12 That ye walk worthy of God, who hath called you unto his kingdom and glory.

Luke 20:34, 35 **34** And Jesus answering said unto them, The children of this world marry, and are given in marriage: **35** But they which shall be accounted worthy to obtain that world, and the resurrection from the dead, neither marry, nor are given in marriage:

The Children of the living God !

Luke 20:36 Neither can they die any more: for they are equal unto the angels; and are the children of God, being the children of the resurrection.

Ephesians 5:1 Be ye therefore followers of God, as dear children;

Ephesians 5:8 For ye were sometimes darkness, but now *are ye* light in the Lord: walk as children of light:

1Thessalonians 5:5 Ye are all the children of light, and the children of the day: we are not of the night, nor of darkness.

Romans 8:1 *There is* therefore now no condemnation to them which are in Christ Jesus, who walk
Read: 8:1 – 39   not after the flesh, but after the Spirit. 2 For the law of the Spirit of life in Christ Jesus hath made me free from the law of sin and death.

Romans 9:26 And it shall come to pass,, *that* in the place where it was said unto them,
Read: 9:2 2- 26   Ye *are* not my people; there shall they be called the children of the living God.

1Peter 1:14 As obedient children, not fashioning yourselves according to the former lusts
Read: 1:1 – 2:25   in your ignorance:

John 14:1 – 3 1 Let not your heart be troubled: ye believe in God, believe also in me. 2 In my Father's house are many
Read: 14:1 – 31   mansions: if *it were* not *so*, I would have told you. I go to prepare a place for you. 3 And if I go and prepare a place for you, I will come again, and receive you unto myself; that where I am, *there* ye may be also.

Teaching and preaching the Gospel of Jesus Christ !

Matthew 28:16 – 20 16 Then the eleven disciples went away into Galilee, into a mountain where Jesus had appointed them. 17 And when they saw him, they worshipped him: but some doubted. 18 And Jesus came and spake unto them, saying, All power is given unto me in heaven and in earth. 19 Go ye therefore, and teach all nations, baptizing them in the name of the Father, and of the Son, and of the Holy Ghost: 20 Teaching them to observe all things whatsoever I have commanded you: and, lo, I am with you alway, *even* unto the end of the world. A-men'.

2Timothy 3:16 – 4:5

1:1 Paul, an apostle of Jesus Christ by the will of God, according to the promise of life which is in Christ Jesus,
3:16,17 16 All scripture *is* given by inspiration of God, and *is* profitable for doctrine, for reproof, for correction, for instruction in righteousness: 17 That the man of God may be perfect, throughly furnished unto all good works.

4:1 – 5 1 I charge *thee* therefore before God, and the Lord Jesus Christ, who shall judge the quick and the dead at his appearing and his kingdom; 2 Preach the word; be instant in season, out of season; reprove, rebuke, exhort with all longsuffering and doctrine.

4:16 – 18 16 At my first answer no man stood with me, but all *men* forsook me: *I pray God* that it may not be laid to their charge. 17 Notwithstanding the Lord stood with me, and strengthened me; that by me the preaching might be fully known, and *that* all the Gentiles might hear: and I was delivered out of the mouth of the lion. 18 And the Lord shall deliver me from every evil work, and will preserve *me* unto his heavenly kingdom: to whom *be* glory for ever and ever. A-men'.

1Corinthians 1:18 For the preaching of the cross is to them that perish foolishness; but unto us which are saved it is the power of God.

1Corinthians 15:58 Therefore, my beloved brethren, be ye stedfast, unmoveable, always abounding in the work of the Lord, forasmuch as ye know that your labour is not in vain in the Lord.

Acts 28:30,31 30 And Paul dwelt two whole years in his own hired house, and received all that came in unto him, 31 Peaching the kingdom of God, and teaching those things which concern the Lord Jesus Christ, with all confidence, no man forbidding him.

Hired, pp. Procured or taken for use, at a stipulated or reasonable price ; as a hired farm .

Read: **Romans 10:4, 8 – 17** ; **Ephesians 4:1 – 7** ; **1Tomothy 6:12 – 16** ; **Romans 8:16,17** ; **Philippians 3:1 – 21** ; **Galatians 3:22 - 29**

Teach, *v.t.*

[...; all implying sending, passing, communicating, or rather leading, drawing.]

1. To instruct; to inform; to communicate to another the knowledge of that of which
he was before ignorant.

2. To deliver any doctrine. (**My note:** *God's holy word;* the **King James Version** *of the Holy Bible*)

3. To tell.

4. To instruct.

5. To show.

6. To make familiar.

7. To inform or admonish.

8. To suggest to the mind.

9. To signify or give notice.

10. To counsel or direct.

We are to do all of the above, as the Holy Spirit leads and directs.

2Timothy 3:16,17 *Read:* **3:16 – 4:5**
16 All scripture *is* given by inspiration of God, and *is* profitable for doctrine,
for reproof, for correction, for instruction in righteousness: 17 That the man of God
may be perfect, throughly furnished unto all good works.

Romans 8:16,17   16 The Spirit itself beareth witness with our spirit, that we are the children of God: 17 And if children,
then heirs; heirs of God, and joint-heirs with Christ; if so be that we suffer with *him*,
that we may be also glorified together.

Read: **Galatians 3:26 – 29 ; 4:6 ,7 ; 1Corinthians 1:23,24 ; Romans 9:26**

My note: <u>All of</u> **the children of God** ; <u>All who are</u> **born again** ; <u>All who are</u> **filled with the Holy Ghost**

SHALL
receive eternal life
SHALL
receive a glorified body
SHALL
dwell with the Lord, FOR EVER !!!

My note: *I am to honour God my Father, in sharing and declaring the gospel of the Lord Jesus Christ,
and <u>in teaching</u> God's holy word* (the K JV of the Holy Bible); *by the leading of and in the power of,*

the holy *Spirit* of God!

Revelation 22:17 – 21

17And the Spirit and the bride say, Come. And let him that heareth say, Come. And let him that is athirst come. And whosoever will, let him take the water of life freely. 18 For I testify unto every man that heareth the words of the prophecy of this book, If any man shall add unto these things, God shall add unto him the plagues that are written in this book: 19 And if any man shall take away from the words of the book of this prophecy, God shall take away his part out of the book of life, and out of the holy city, and *from* the things which are written in this book. 20 He which testifieth these things saith, **Surely I come quickly**. A-men'.

Even so, come, Lord Jesus.

21 The grace of our Lord Jesus Christ *be* with you all.

A-men'.

My Personal notes:

Additional Scriptural References

His work in preserving His written word
from:
Pages 28 & 29

My Personal notes:

Read: **Exodus 20:1 - 24:7**

Exodus 24:12   And the LORD said unto Moses, Come up to me into the mount, and be there:
and I will give thee tables of stone, and a law, and commandments <u>which I have written</u>;
that thou mayest teach them.

Exodus 31:18   And he gave unto Moses, when he had made an end of communing with him upon mount Sinai,
<u>two tables of testimony</u>, tables of stone, <u>written with the finger of God</u>.

Exodus 32:15,16   15 And Moses turned, and went down from the mount, and <u>the two tables of the testimony</u> *were* in his
hand: the tables *were* written on both their sides; on the one side and on the other *were* they written.
16 And the tables were the work of God, and <u>the writing was the writing of God</u>, graven upon the tables.

Exodus 32:19   And it came to pass, as soon as he came nigh unto the camp, that he saw the calf, and the dancing:
and Moses' anger waxed hot, and <u>he cast the tables out of his hands</u>, <u>and brake them beneath the mount</u>.

Exodus 34:1   <u>And the LORD said unto Moses, Hew thee two tables of stone like unto the first</u>:
<u>and I will write upon</u> *these* <u>tables the words that were in the first tables</u>, which thou brakest.

Exodus 34:27-29   27 And the LORD said unto <u>Moses, Write thou these words</u>: for after the tenor of these words I have made a
covenant with thee and with Israel. 28 And <u>he</u> was there with the LORD forty days and forty nights;
he did neither eat bread, nor drink water. And <u>he wrote upon the tables the words of the covenant</u>,
<u>the ten commandments</u>. 29 And it came to pass, when Moses came down from mount Sinai with
<u>the two tables of testimony</u> in Moses' hand, when he came down from the mount,
that Moses wist not that the skin of his face shone while he talked with him.

My note: The <u>ten commandments</u> *is the* <u>covenant of the LORD</u> *and the* <u>covenant of the LORD</u> *is the* <u>testimony</u>
of the LORD; which is the Ten Commandments, *and it was put into* <u>the ark of the covenant of the LORD</u> .

Exodus 40:20   <u>And he took and put the testimony into the ark</u>, and set the staves on the ark,
and put the mercy seat above upon the ark:

Deuteronomy 9:9,10,11   9 When I was gone up into the mount to receive <u>the tables of stone</u>, *even* <u>the tables of the covenant</u>
which the LORD made with you, then I abode in the mount forty days and forty nights, I neither
did eat bread nor drink water: 10 And the LORD delivered unto me two tables of stone written
with the finger of God; and on them *was written* according to all the words, which the LORD spake
with you in the mount out of the midst of the fire in the day of the assembly. 11 And it came to
pass at the end of forty days and forty nights, *that* the LORD gave me the two <u>tables of stone</u>,
even <u>the tables of the covenant</u>.

Deuteronomy 29:9   Keep therefore the words of <u>this covenant</u>, and do them, that ye may prosper in all that ye do.

Deuteronomy 31:24-26   24 And it came to pass, <u>when Moses had made an end of writing the words of this law in a book</u>,
until they were finished, 25 That Moses commanded the Levites, which bare <u>the ark of the</u>
<u>covenant of the LORD</u>, saying, 26 <u>Take this book of the law</u>, <u>and put it in the side of the ark of the</u>
<u>covenant of the LORD your God</u>, that it may be there for a witness against thee.

Matthew 22:36-40   36 Master, which *is* the <u>commandment in the law</u>? 37 Jesus said unto him, Thou shalt love the Lord
thy God with all thy heart, and with all thy soul, and with all thy mind. 38 This is the first and
great commandment. 39 And the second is like unto it, Thou shalt love thy neighbour as thyself.
40 <u>On these two commandments</u> hang all the law and the prophets.

Mark 10:18   And Jesus said unto him, Why callest thou me good? *there is* none good but one, *that is*, God. 19 Thou knowest
the commandments, Do not commit adultery, Do not kill, Do not steal, Do not bear false witness, Defraud not,
Honour thy father and mother.

My note: The <u>ten commandments</u> *given to Moses by the LORD were preserved unto the days of Jesus and Jesus declared them as,*
absolute truth from God HIS Father ; recognizing these men as the servants of the LORD, who the LORD delivered them unto,
for HIS people.

His work in preserving His written word
Additional Scriptural References
continued...
This Scripture was fulfilled.

Read: **Hebrews 8:1 – 10:18**

Hebrews 10:7 Then said I, Lo, I come (in the volume of the book it is written of me,) to do thy will, O God.

Hebrews 10:16 This *is* the covenant that I will make with them after those days, saith the Lord, I will put my laws
into their hearts, and in their minds will I write them; **17** And their sins and iniquities will I remember no more.
18 Now were remission of these *is, there is* no more offering for sin.

Jeremiah 30:1,2 **1** The word that came to Jeremiah from the LORD, saying, **2** Thus speaketh the LORD God of Israel, saying,
Write thee all the words that I have spoken unto thee in a book.

Jeremiah 31:33,34 **33** But this *shall be* the covenant that I will make with the house of Israel; After those days, saith the LORD,
I will put my law in their inward parts, and write it in their hearts; and will be their God, and they shall be
my people. **34** And they shall teach no more every man his neighbour, and every man his brother, saying,
Know the LORD: for they shall all know me, from the least of them unto the greatest of them,
saith the LORD: for I will forgive them their iniquity, and I will remember their sin no more.

Jeremiah 36:1,2 **1** And it came to pass in the fourth year of Jehoiakim the son of Josiah king of Judah, *that* this word came
unto Jeremiah from the LORD, saying, **2** Take thee a roll of a book, and write therein all the words
that I have spoken unto thee against Israel, and against Judah, and against all the nations,
from the day I spake unto thee, from the days of Josiah, even unto this day.

Revelation 1:1-3 **1** The Revelation of Jesus Christ, which God gave unto him, to shew unto his servants things which must
shortly come to pass; and he sent and signified *it* by his angel unto his servant John: **2** Who bare record of
the word of God, and of the testimony of Jesus Christ, and of all things that he saw. **3** Blessed *is* he that
readeth, and they that hear the words of this prophecy, and keep those things which are written therein:
for the time *is* at hand.

Revelation 1:9-11 **9** I John, who also am your brother, and companion in tribulation, and in the kingdom and patience of
Jesus Christ, was in the isle that is called Patmos, for the word of God, and for the testimony of Jesus Christ.
10 I was in the Spirit on the Lord's day, and heard behind me a great voice, as of a trumpet. **11** Saying,
I am Alpha and Omega, the first and the last: and, What thou seest, write in a book, and send *it* unto the
seven churches which are in Asia; unto Ephesus, and unto Smyrna, and unto Pergamos, and unto
Thyatira, and unto Sardis, and unto Philadelphia, and unto Laodicea.

Revelation 14:13 And I heard a voice from heaven saying unto me, Write, Blessed *are* the dead which die in the Lord from
henceforth: Yea, saith the Spirit, that they may rest from their labours; and their works do follow them.

Revelation 19:9 And he saith unto me, Write, Blessed *are* they which are called unto the marriage supper of the Lamb.
And he saith unto me, These are the true sayings of God.

Revelation 21:5 And he that sat upon the throne said, Behold, I make all things new. And he said unto me, Write:
for these words are true and faithful.

His work in preserving His written word
Additional Scriptural References
continued...
This Scripture was fulfilled.

Adam, n. ... ; primarily, the name of the human species, mankind ; appropriately, the first Man, the progenitor of the human race.
The word signifies form, shape, or suitable form ; hence, species. ... It is evidently connected with ... damah, Heb.
Ch. Syr. , to be like or equal, to form an image, to assimilate. Whence the sense of likeness, image, form, shape;

*Quickening , ppr. **Giving life ;***

1Corinthians 15:45 And so it is written, The first man Adam was made a living soul; the last Adam *was made* a quickening spirit.
Read: 15:45 - 47

Genesis 1:27 So God created man in his *own* image, in the image of God created he him; male and female created he them.

Genesis 2:7 And the LORD God formed man *of* the dust of the ground, and breathed into his nostrils the breath of life;
and man became a living soul.

Genesis 5:1 This *is* the book of the generations of Adam. In the day that God created man, in the likeness of God made he him;

His work in preserving His written word
Additional Scriptural References
continued...
This Scripture was fulfilled.

1Corinthians 15:54 54 So when this corruptible shall have put on incorruption, and this mortal shall have put on immortality, then shall be brought to pass the saying that is written, Death is swallowed up in victory. **55** O death, where *is* thy sting? O grave, where *is* thy victory? **56** The sting of death *is* sin; and the strength of sin *is* the law. **57** But thanks *be* to God, which giveth us the victory through our Lord Jesus Christ.

Isaiah 25:8 He will swallow up death in victory; and the Lord GOD will wipe away tears from off all faces; and the rebuke of his people shall he take away from off all the earth: for the LORD hath spoken *it*.

1Peter 1:16 Because it is written, Be ye holy; for I am holy.

Leviticus 19:1,2 1 And the LORD spake unto Moses, saying, **2** Speak unto all the congregation of the children of Israel, and say unto them, Ye shall be holy: for I the LORD your God *am* holy.

His work in preserving His written word
Additional Scriptural References
continued...
This Scripture was fulfilled.

Habakkuk 2:4 Behold, his soul *which* is lifted up is not upright in him: but the just shall live by his faith.

Acts 13:39 And by him all that believe are justified from all things, from which ye could not be justified by the law of Moses.

Romans 1:17 For therein is the righteousness of God revealed from faith to faith: as it is written, The just shall live by faith.

Galatians 3:11 But that no man is justified by the law in the sight of God, *it is* evident: for, The just shall live by faith.

Hebrews 10:38 Now the just shall live by faith: but if *any man* draw back, my soul shall have no pleasure in him.

His work in preserving His written word
Additional Scriptural References
continued...
This Scripture was fulfilled.

Isaiah 53:5 But he *was* wounded for our transgressions, *he was* bruised for our iniquities: the chastisement of our peace *was* upon him; and with his stripes we are healed.

1Peter 2:23 Who, when he was reviled, reviled not again; when he suffered, he threatened not; but committed *himself* to him that judgeth righteously:

1Peter 2:24 Who his own self bare our sins in his own body on the tree, that we, being dead to sins, should live unto righteousness: by whose stripes ye were healed.

1Peter 2:25 For ye were as sheep going astray; but are now returned unto the Shepherd and Bishop of your souls.

Isaiah 53:6 All we like sheep have gone astray; we have turned every one to his own way; and the LORD hath laid on him the iniquity of us all. **7** He was oppressed, and he was afflicted, yet he opened not his mouth: he is brought as a lamb to the slaughter, and as a sheep before her shearers is dumb, so he openeth not his mouth.

His work in preserving His written word
Additional Scriptural References
continued...
This Scripture was fulfilled.

John 19:37 And again another scripture saith, They shall look on him whom they pierced.

Zechariah 12:10 ... : and they shall look upon me whom they have pierced, ...

Zechariah 13:6 And *one* shall say unto him, What *are* these wounds in thine hands? Then he shall answer, *Those* with which I was wounded *in* the house of my friends.

Psalm 22:16 For dogs have compassed me: the assembly of the wicked have inclosed me: they pierced my hands and my feet.

Psalm 22:17 I may tell all my bones: they look *and* stare upon me.

His work in preserving His written word
Additional Scriptural References
<u>*continued...*</u>
This Scripture was fulfilled.

Psalm 41:9 Yea, <u>mine own familiar friend</u>, in whom I trusted, <u>which did eat of my bread</u>, <u>hath lifted up</u> *his* <u>heel against me</u>.

Matthew 26:14-25 **14** Then one of the twelve, called Judas Iscariot, went unto the chief priests, **15** And said *unto them*, What will ye give me, and I will deliver him unto you? And they covenanted with him for thirty pieces of silver. **16** And from that time he sought opportunity to betray him. **17** Now <u>the first</u> *day* of the *feast of unleavened* bread the disciples came to Jesus, saying unto him, Where wilt thou that we prepare for thee to eat the passover? **18** And he said, Go into the city to such a man, and say unto him, The Master saith, My time is at hand; I will keep the passover at thy house with my disciples. **19** And the disciples did as Jesus had appointed them; and <u>they made ready the passover</u>. **20** Now <u>when the even was come</u>, he sat down with the twelve. **21** And <u>as they did eat</u>, he said, Verily I say unto you, that one of you shall betray me. **22** And they were exceeding sorrowful, and began every one of them to say unto him, Lord, is it I ? **23** And he answered and said, He that dippeth *his* hand with me in the dish, the same shall betray me. **24** The Son of man goeth as it is written of him: but woe unto that man by whom the Son of man is betrayed! it had been good for that man if he had not been born. **25** Then Judas, which betrayed him, answered and said, Master, is it I ? He said unto him, Thou hast said.

Matthew 26:45-56 **45** Then cometh he to his disciples, and saith unto them, Sleep on now, and take *your* rest: behold, the hour is at hand, and the Son of man is betrayed into the hands of sinners. **46** Rise, let us be going: behold, he is at hand that doth betray me. **47** And while he yet spake, lo, <u>Judas</u>, <u>one of the twelve</u>, came, and with him <u>a great multitude with swords</u> and staves, from the chief priests and elders of the people. **48** Now <u>he that betrayed him</u> gave them a sign, saying, Whomsoever I shall kiss, that same is he: hold him fast. **49** And forthwith <u>he came to Jesus</u>, <u>and said</u>, Hail, master; <u>and kissed him</u>. **50** <u>And Jesus said unto him</u>, Friend, wherefore art thou come? Then came they, and laid hands on Jesus, and took him. **51** And, behold, one of them which were with Jesus stretched out *his* hand, and drew his sword, and struck a servant of the high priest's, and smote off his ear. **52** Then said Jesus unto him, Put up again thy sword into his place: for all they that take the sword shall perish with the sword. **53** Thinkest thou that I cannot now pray to my Father, and he shall presently give me more than twelve legions of angels? **54** But <u>how then shall the scriptures be fulfilled</u>, <u>that thus it must be</u>? **55** In that same hour said Jesus to the multitudes, Are ye come out as against a thief <u>with swords</u> and staves for to take me? I sat daily with you teaching in the temple, and ye laid no hold on me. **56** But all this was done, that <u>the scriptures of the prophets might be fulfilled</u>. <u>Then all the disciples forsook him, and fled</u>.

Zechariah 13:7 Awake, O sword, <u>against my shepherd</u>, and against the man *that is* my fellow, saith the LORD of hosts: <u>smite the shepherd</u>, <u>and the sheep shall be scattered</u>: and I will turn mine hand upon the little ones.

Read: **Matthew 26:31**
Read: **Mark 14:27**

His work in preserving His written word
Additional Scriptural References
<u>*continued...*</u>
This Scripture was fulfilled.

John 19:30 When Jesus therefore had received the vinegar, he said, It is finished: and he bowed his head, and gave up the ghost. **31** The Jews therefore, because it was the preparation, that the bodies should not remain upon the cross on the Sabbath day, (for that sabbath day was an high day,) besought Pilate that their legs might be broken, and *that* they might be taken away. **32** Then came the soldiers, and brake the legs of the first, and of the other which was crucified with him. **33** But <u>when they came to Jesus</u>, and <u>saw that he was dead already</u> <u>they</u>, <u>brake not his legs</u>: **34** But one of the soldiers with a spear pierced his side, and forthwith came there out blood and water. **35** And he that *saw it* bare record, and his record is true: and he knoweth that he saith true, that ye might believe.

John 19:36 For these things were done, that <u>the scripture should be fulfilled</u>, <u>A bone of him shall not be broken</u>.

Psalm 34:20 He keepeth all his bones: <u>not one of them is broken</u>.

Exodus 12:46 In the house shall it be eaten; thou shalt not carry forth ought of the flesh abroad out of the house;
Read: **12:1 – 11 ; 21 ; 42, 43**
<u>neither shall ye break a bone thereof</u>.

Numbers 9:12 They shall leave none of it unto the morning, <u>nor break any bone of it</u>: according to all the ordinances of the passover they shall keep it.

My note: " of it: " *of the lamb*

His work in preserving His written word
Additional Scriptural References
continued...
This Scripture was fulfilled.

Psalm 69:21   They gave me also gall for my meat; and in my thirst they gave me vinegar to drink.

Matthew 27:34   They gave him vinegar to drink mingled with gall: and when he had tasted *thereof*, he would not drink.

Psalm 22:18   They part my garments among them, and cast lots upon my vesture.

Matthew 27:35   And they crucified him, and parted his garments, casting lots: that it might be fulfilled which was spoken by the prophet, They parted my garments among them, and upon my vesture did they cast lots.

John 19:23,24   23 Then the soldiers, when they had crucified Jesus, took his garments, and made four parts, to every soldier a part; and also *his* coat: now the coat was without seam, woven from the top throughout. 24 They said therefore among themselves, Let us not rend it, but cast lots for it, whose it shall be: that the scripture might be fulfilled, which saith, They parted my raiment among them, and for my vesture they did cast lots.

These things therefore the soldiers did.

His work in preserving His written word
Additional Scriptural References
continued...
This Scripture was fulfilled.

Psalm 22:7   All they that see me laugh me to scorn: they shoot out the lip, they shake the head, *saying*,

Psalm 22:8   He trusted on the LORD *that* he would deliver him: let him deliver him, seeing he delighted in him.

Mark 15:20   16 And the soldiers led him away into the hall, called Praetorium; and they call together the whole band.
17 And they clothed him with purple, and platted a crown of thorns, and put it about his *head*,
18 And began to salute him, Hail, King of the Jews! 19 And they smote him on the head with a reed, and did spit upon him, and bowing *their* knees worshipped him. 20 And when they had mocked him, they took off the purple from him, and put his own clothes on him, and led him out to crucify him.

Matthew 27:39   And they that passed by reviled him, wagging their heads, 40 And saying, Thou that destroyest the temple, and buildest *it* in three days, save thyself. If thou be the Son of God, come down from the cross.

Matthew 27:43   He trusted in God; let him deliver him now, if he will have him: for he said, I am the Son of God.

His work in preserving His written word
Additional Scriptural References
continued...
This Scripture was fulfilled.

Luke 4:17-20   17 And there was delivered unto him the book of the prophet Esaias. And when he had opened the book, he found the place where it was written, 18 The Spirit of the Lord *is* upon me, because he hath anointed me to preach the gospel to the poor; he hath sent me to heal the brokenhearted, to preach deliverance to the captives, and recovering of sight to the blind, to set at liberty them that are bruised, 19 To preach the acceptable year of the Lord. 20 And he closed the book, and he gave *it* again to the minister, and sat down. And the eyes of all them that were in the synagogue were fastened on him. 21 And he began to say unto them, This day is this scripture fulfilled in your ears.

Isaiah 61:1,2   1 The Spirit of the Lord GOD *is* upon me; because the LORD hath anointed me to preach good tidings unto the meek; he hath sent me to bind up the brokenhearted, to proclaim liberty to the captives, and the opening of the prison to *them that are* bound; 2 To proclaim the acceptable year of the LORD, and the day of vengeance of our God; to comfort all that mourn;

His work in preserving His written word
Additional Scriptural References
continued…
This Scripture was fulfilled.

Matthew 3:1-4 1 In those days came John the Baptist, preaching in the wilderness of Judaea, 2 And saying, Repent ye: for the kingdom of heaven is at hand. 3 For this is he that was spoken of by the prophet Esaias, saying, The voice of one crying in the wilderness, Prepare ye the way of the Lord, make his paths straight.

4 And the same John had his raiment of camel's hair, and a leathern girdle about his loins; and his meat was locusts and wild honey. 5 Then went out to him Jerusalem, and all Judaea, and all the region round about Jordan, 6 And were baptized of him in Jordan, confessing their sins.

Isaiah 40:3 The voice of him that crieth in the wilderness, Prepare ye the way of the LORD, make straight in the desert a highway for our God.

Matthew 11:13,14 13 For all the prophets and the law prophesied until John. 14 And if ye will receive it, this is Elias, which was for to come.

My note: Isaiah prophesied the word of the LORD ; " Prepare ye the way of the LORD, " ; fulfilled by John the Baptist.

Matthew 11:9,10 9 But what went ye out for to see? A prophet? yea, I say unto you, and more than a prophet. 10 For this is *he*, of whom it is written, Behold, I send my messenger before thy face, which shall prepare thy way before thee.

Malachi 3:1 Behold, I will send my messenger, and he shall prepare the way before me: and the Lord, whom ye seek, shall suddenly come to his temple, even the messenger of the covenant, whom ye delight in: behold, he shall come, saith the LORD of hosts.

Mark 1:1-8 1 The beginning of the gospel of Jesus Christ, the Son of God; 2 As it is written in the prophets, Behold, I send my messenger before thy face, which shall prepare thy way before thee. 3 The voice of one crying in the wilderness, Prepare ye the way of the Lord, make his paths straight. 4 John did baptize in the wilderness, and preach the baptism of repentance for the remission of sins. 5 And there went out unto him all the land of Judaea, and they of Jerusalem, and were all baptized of him in the river of Jordan, confessing their sins. 6 And John was clothed with camel's hair, and with a girdle of a skin about his loins; and he did eat locusts and wild honey; 7 And preached, saying, There cometh one mightier than I after me, the latchet of whose shoes I am not worthy to stoop down and unloose. 8 I indeed have baptized you with water: but he shall baptize you with the Holy Ghost.

Luke 1:13 But the angel said unto him, Fear not, Zacharias: for thy prayer is heard; and thy wife Elizabeth shall bear thee a son, and thou shalt call his name John. 14 And thou shalt have joy and gladness; and many shall rejoice at his birth. 15 For he shall be great in the sight of the Lord, and shall drink neither wine nor strong drink; and he shall be filled with the Holy Ghost, even from his mother's womb. 16 And many of the children of Israel shall he turn to the Lord their God. 17 And he shall go before him in the spirit and power of Elias, to turn the hearts of the fathers to the children, and the disobedient to the wisdom of the just; to make ready a people prepared for the Lord.

Luke 3:4 As it is written in the book of the words of Esaias the prophet, saying, The voice of one crying in the wilderness, Prepare ye the way of the Lord, make his paths straight.

John 1:19-23 19 And this is the record of John, when the Jews sent priests and Levites from Jerusalem to ask him, Who art thou? 20 And he confessed, and denied not; but confessed, I am not the Christ. 21 And they asked him, What then? Art thou Elias? And he saith, I am not. Art thou that prophet? And he answered, No. 22 Then said they unto him, Who art thou? that we may give an answer to them that sent us. What sayest thou of thyself? 23 He said, I *am* the voice of one crying in the wilderness, Make straight the way of the Lord, as said the prophet Esaias.

Psalm 2:7 I will declare the decree: the LORD hath said unto me, Thou *art* my Son; this day have I begotten thee.

John 1:14 And the Word was made flesh, and dwelt among us, (and we beheld his glory, the glory as of the only begotten of the Father,) full of grace and truth.

John 1:18 No man hath seen God at any time; the only begotten Son, which is in the bosom of the Father, he hath declared *him*.

John 3:16-18 16 For God so loved the world, that he gave his only begotten Son, that whosoever believeth in him should not perish, but have everlasting life. 17 For God sent not his Son into the world to condemn the world; but that the world through him might be saved. 18 He that believeth on him is not condemned: but he that believeth not is condemned already, because he hath not believed in the name of the only begotten Son of God.

Hebrews 1:5 For unto which of the angels said he at any time, Thou art my Son, this day have I begotten thee? And again, I will be to him a Father, and he shall be to me a Son?

Matthew 3;17 And lo a voice from heaven, saying, This is my beloved Son, in whom I am well pleased.

Mark 1:11 And there came a voice from heaven, *saying*, Thou art my beloved Son, in whom I am well pleased.

Mark 9:7 And there was a cloud that overshadowed them: and a voice came out of the cloud, saying, This is my beloved Son: hear him.

Luke 3:22 And the Holy Ghost descending in a bodily shape like a dove upon him, and a voice came from heaven, which said, Thou art my beloved Son; in thee I am well pleased.

Acts 13:33 God hath fulfilled the same unto us their children, in that he hath raised up Jesus again; as it is also written in the second psalm, Thou art my Son, this day have I begotten thee.

His work in preserving His written word

Additional Scriptural References

continued…

This Scripture was fulfilled.

My note: *The assembly gathered around Jesus and had a part in the slaying of the passover lamb, which was to be done at night; so, God darkened the earth as night, while Jesus was slain and killed; which fulfilled scripture.* **Exodus 12:1-3, 6, 8, 10**

John 19:14 And it was the preparation of the passover, and about the sixth hour: and he saith unto the Jews, Behold your King!

Matthew 27:45 Now from the sixth hour there was darkness over all the land unto the ninth hour. 46 And about the ninth hour Jesus cried with a loud voice, saying, Eli, Eli, lama sabachthani? that is to say, My God, my God, why hast thou forsaken me?

Matthew 27:50 Jesus, when he had cried again with a loud voice, yielded up the ghost. 51 And, behold, the veil of the temple was rent in twain from the top to the bottom; and the earth did quake, and the rocks rent;

Mark 15:33 And when the sixth hour was come, there was darkness over the whole land until the ninth hour. 34 And at the ninth hour Jesus cried with a loud voice, saying, Eloi, Eloi, lama sabachthani? which is, being interpreted, My God, my God, why hast thou forsaken me?

Mark 15:37 And Jesus cried with a loud voice, and gave up the ghost.

Luke 23:44 And it was about the sixth hour, and there was a darkness over all the earth until the ninth hour. 45 And the sun was darkened, and the veil of the temple was rent in the midst. 46 And when Jesus had cried with a loud voice, he said, Father, into thy hands I commend my spirit: and having said thus, he gave up the ghost.

Read: **John 19:30 – 42** 31 The Jews therefore, because it was the preparation, that the bodies should not remain upon the cross on the sabbath day, (for that sabbath day was an high day,) besought Pilate that their legs might be broken, and *that* they might be taken away.

Deuteronomy 21:22,23 23 His body shall not remain all night upon the tree, but thou shalt in any wise bury him that day; …

My note: *The body of Jesus was removed that same day; HE did not remain upon the cross until the morning: All was fulfilled.*

His work in preserving His written word
Additional Scriptural References
continued...
This Scripture was fulfilled.

Psalm 16:10 For thou wilt not leave my soul in hell;

neither wilt thou suffer thine Holy One to see corruption.

Acts 2:21-36 21 And it shall come to pass, *that* whosoever shall call on the name of the Lord shall be saved. **22** Ye men of Israel,, hear these words; Jesus of Nazareth, a man approved of God among you by miracles and wonders and signs, which God did by him in the midst of you, as ye yourselves also know: **23** Him, being delivered by the determinate counsel and foreknowledge of God, ye have taken, and by wicked hands have crucified and slain: **24** Whom God hath raised up, having loosed the pains of death: because it was not possible that he should be holden of it. **25** For David speaking concerning him, I foresaw the Lord always before my face, for he is on my right hand, that I should not be moved: **26** Therefore did my heart rejoice, and my tongue was glad; moreover also my flesh shall rest in hope: **27** Because thou wilt not leave my soul in hell, neither wilt thou suffer thine Holy One to see corruption. **28** Thou hast made known to me the ways of life; thou shalt make me full of joy with thy countenance. **29** Men *and* brethren, let me freely speak unto you of the patriarch David, that he is both dead and buried, and his sepulchre is with us unto this day. **30** Therefore being a prophet, and knowing that God had sworn with an oath to him, that of the fruit of his loins, according to the flesh, he would raise up Christ to sit on his throne;

Acts 13:16 Then Paul stood up, and beckoning with *his* hand said, Men of Israel, and ye that fear God, give audience.

Acts 13:29 And when they had fulfilled all that was written of him, they took *him* down from the tree, and laid *him* in a sepulchre. **30** But God raised him from the dead:

Acts 13:33 God hath fulfilled the same unto us their children, in that he hath raised up Jesus again; as it is also written in the second psalm, Thou art my Son, this day have I begotten thee. **34** And also concerning that he raised him up from the dead, *now* no more to return to corruption, he said on this wise, I will give you the sure mercies of David. **35** Wherefore he saith also in another *psalm*, Thou shalt not suffer thine Holy One to see corruption. **36** For David, after he had served his own generation by the will of God, fell on sleep, and was laid unto his fathers, and saw corruption: **37** But he, whom God raised again, saw no corruption.

Matthew 16:21 From that time forth began Jesus to shew unto his disciples, how that he must go unto Jerusalem, and suffer many things of the elders and chief priests and scribes, and be killed, and be raised again the third day.

Matthew 17:22,23 22 And while they abode in Galilee, Jesus said unto them, The Son of man shall be betrayed into the hands of men: 23 And they shall kill him, and the third day he shall be raised again. And they were exceeding sorry.

Matthew 20:17-19 17 And Jesus going up to Jerusalem took the twelve disciples apart in the way, and said unto them, 18 Behold, we go up to Jerusalem; and the Son of man shall be betrayed unto the chief priests and unto the scribes, and they shall condemn him to death, 19 And shall deliver him to the Gentiles to mock, and to scourge, and to crucify *him*: and the third day he shall rise again.

Matthew 27:62-64 62 Now the next day, that followed the day of the preparation, the chief priests and Pharisees came together unto Pilate, 63 Saying, Sir, we remember that that deceiver said, while he was yet alive, After three days I will rise again. 64 Command therefore that the sepulchre be made sure until the third day, lest his disciples come by night, and steal him away, and say unto the people, He is risen from the dead: so the last error shall be worse than the first.

Mark 9:31 For he taught his disciples, and said unto them, The Son of man is delivered into the hands of men, and they shall kill him; and after that he is killed, he shall rise the third day.

Mark 10:34 32 And they were in the way going up to Jerusalem; and Jesus went before them: and they were amazed; and as they followed, they were afraid. And he took again the twelve, and began to tell them what things should happen unto him, 33 *Saying*, Behold, we go to Jerusalem; and the Son of man shall be delivered unto the chief priests, and unto the scribes; and they shall condemn him to death, and shall deliver him to the Gentiles: 34 And they shall mock him, and shall scourge him, and shall spit upon him, and shall kill him: and the third day he shall rise again.

Luke 9:22 Saying, The Son of man must suffer many things, and be rejected of the elders and chief priests and scribes, and be slain, and be raised the third day.

Psalm 16:10 For thou wilt not leave my soul in hell;

neither wilt thou suffer thine Holy One to see corruption.

Luke 18:33 31 Then he took *unto him* the twelve, and said unto them, Behold, we go up to Jerusalem, and all things that are written by the prophets concerning the Son of man shall be accomplished. 32 For he shall be delivered unto the Gentiles, and shall be mocked, and spitefully entreated, and spitted on: 33 And they shall scourge *him*, and put him to death: and the third day he shall rise again.

Read: Luke 24:1 - 53
Luke 24:7 6 He is not here, but is risen: remember how he spake unto you when he was yet in Galilee, 7 Saying, The Son of man must be delivered into the hands of sinful men, and be crucified, and the third day rise again. 8 And they remembered his words,

Luke 24:38,39 38 And he said unto them, Why are ye troubled? and why do thoughts arise in your hearts? 39 Behold my hands and my feet, that it is I myself: handle me, and see; for a spirit hath not flesh and bones, as ye see me have.

Luke 24:46 44 And he said unto them, These *are* the words which I spake unto you, while I was yet with you, that all things must be fulfilled, which were written in the law of Moses, and *in* the prophets, and *in* the psalms, concerning me. 45 Then opened he their understanding, that they might understand the scriptures, 46 And said unto them, Thus it is written, and thus it behoved Christ to suffer, and to rise from the dead the third day:

Acts 10:38, 39, 40 38 How God anointed Jesus of Nazareth with the Holy Ghost and with power: who went about doing good, and healing all that were oppressed of the devil; for God was with him. 39 And we are witnesses of all things which he did both in the land of the Jews, and in Jerusalem; whom they slew and hanged on a tree: 40 Him God raised up the third day, and shewed him openly;

1Corinthians 15:4 1 Moreover, brethren, I declare unto you the gospel which I preached unto you, which also ye have received, and wherein ye stand; 2 By which also ye are saved, if ye keep in memory what I preached unto you, unless ye have believed in vain. 3 For I delivered unto you first of all that which I also received, how that Christ died for our sins according to the scriptures; 4 And that he was buried, and that he rose again the third day according to the scriptures:

His work in preserving His written word
Additional Scriptural References
continued...

2Timothy 3:14 – 17 14 But continue thou in the things which thou hast learned and hast been assured of, knowing of whom thou hast learned *them*; 15 And that from a child thou hast known the holy scriptures, which are able to make thee wise unto salvation through faith which is in Christ Jesus. 16 All scripture *is* given by inspiration of God, and *is* profitable for doctrine, for reproof, for correction, for instruction in righteousness: 17 That the man of God may be perfect, throughly furnished unto all good works.

Psalm 23:1 – 6 1 The LORD *is* my shepherd; I shall not want. 2 He maketh me to lie down in green pastures: he leadeth me beside the still waters. 3 He restoreth my soul: he leadeth me in the paths of righteousness for his name's sake. 4 Yea, though I walk through the valley of the shadow of death, I will fear no evil: for thou *art* with me; thy rod and thy staff they comfort me. 5 Thou preparest a table before me in the presence of mine enemies: thou anointest my head with oil; my cup runneth over. 6 Surely goodness and mercy shall follow me all the days of my life: and I will dwell in the house of the LORD for ever.

Revelation 22:20, 21 20 He which testifieth these things saith, Surely I come quickly. A-men'. Even so, come, Lord Jesus. 21 The grace of our Lord Jesus Christ *be* with you all. A-men'.

<u>*My Personal notes:*</u>

Additional Scriptural References

Symbols of the Holy Spirit's actions
from:
Pages 38 & 39

My Personal notes:

Oil

Noah Webster 1828
American Dictionary of the English Language

Unction, n. *[..., to anoint.]* *The act of anointing.* *7. Divine or sanctifying grace.* **1John i i .** vs.20

My note: anoint = sanctify

Anoint, *v.t.* *2. To* consecrate *by* unction, *or the use of oil.*

4. To prepare, in allusion *to the consecrating use of oil.*

Thou shalt anoint the alter, and sanctify it. **Ex. xxix .**

My note: Sanctified is defined on page 111

Anoint the shield. **Isaiah xxi .**

To anoint the head with oil, **Ps. 23:5**, *seems to signify to communicate the* consolation *of the Holy Spirit.*

My note: Consolation is defined on page 111

Webster's note: *The use of oil in consecrations, was of high antiquity. Kings, prophets and priests were set apart or consecrated to their offices by the use of oil. Hence the peculiar application of the term anointed to Jesus Christ.*

Antiquity , n. *1. Ancient times ; former ages ; times long since past ;*

Allusion, *n. A reference to something not explicitly mentioned ;*

Allude , *v.i. To refer to something not directly mentioned ;*

Consecrate, *v.t. [... see sacred.] 1. To make or declare to be sacred, by certain ceremonies or rites; to appropriate to sacred uses; to set apart, dedicate, or devote, to the service and worship of God; as, to consecrate a church.* **Ex. xxix ; Josh. vi .**

Exodus 25:1 And the LORD spake unto Moses, saying, …

Exodus 29:1 And this *is* the thing that thou shalt do unto them to hallow them, to minister unto me in the priest's office:
My note: " them *" is Aaron and his sons*
Take one young bullock, and two rams without blemish.

Exodus 29:7 Then shalt thou take the anointing oil, and pour *it* upon his head, and anoint him. *My note:" him" = Aaron*

Exodus 29:21 And thou shalt take of the blood that *is* upon the altar, and of the anointing oil, and sprinkle *it* upon Aaron, and upon his garments, and upon his sons, and upon the garments of his sons with him: and he shall be hallowed, and his garments, and his sons, and his sons' garments with him.

Leviticus
8:30 And Moses took of the anointing oil, and of the blood which *was* upon the altar, and sprinkled *it* upon Aaron, *and* upon his garments, and upon his sons, and upon his son's garments with him; and sanctified Aaron, *and* his garments, and his sons, and his sons' garments with him.

21:10 And *he that is* the high priest among his brethren, upon whose head the anointing oil was poured, and that is consecrated to put on the garments, shall not uncover his head, nor rend his clothes;

21:12 Neither shall he go out of the sanctuary, nor profane the sanctuary of his God; for the crown of the anointing oil of his God *is* upon him: I *am* the LORD.

Psalms
89:20,21, 26
89:25 - 29
20 I have found David my servant; with my holy oil have I anointed him:
21 With whom my hand shall be established: mine arm also shall strengthen him.

26 He shall cry unto me, Thou *art* my father, my God, and the rock of my salvation.

Psalm
23:1 – 6 **5** Thou preparest a table before me in the presence of mine enemies: thou anointest my head with oil;
my cup runneth over.

Isaiah 61:3   **1** The Spirit of the Lord GOD *is* upon me; because the LORD hath anointed me to preach good tidings upon the meek; he hath sent me to bind up the brokenhearted, to proclaim liberty to the captives, and the opening of the prison to *them that are* bound; **2** To proclaim the acceptable year of the LORD, and the day of vengeance of our God; to comfort all that mourn; **3** To appoint unto them that mourn in Zion, to give unto them beauty for ashes, the oil of joy for mourning, the garment of praise for the spirit of heaviness; that they might be called trees of righteousness, the planting of the LORD, that he might be glorified.

Oil

Anointed, n. The <u>Messiah</u>, or <u>Son of God</u>, consecrated to the great office of <u>Redeemer</u>; called <u>the Lord's anointed</u>.

Cyrus is also called the Lord's anointed. **Isaiah xlv .**

Anointed, pp. <u>Smeared or rubbed with oil</u> ; <u>set apart</u> ; <u>consecrated with oil</u> .

<u>*My note*</u>: *anoint = to smear or rub on.*

Mark 6:13 And they cast out many devils, and <u>anointed with oil</u> <u>many that were sick</u>, and healed *them*.

Luke 7:46 44 And he turned to the woman, and said unto Simon, Seest thou this woman? I entered into thine house, thou gavest me no water for my feet: but she hath washed my feet with tears, and wiped *them* with the hairs of her head. 45 Thou gavest me no kiss: but this woman since the time I came in hath not ceased to kiss my feet. 46 <u>My head with oil thou didst not anoint</u>: but <u>this woman hath</u> <u>anointed my feet with ointment</u>. 47 Wherefore I say unto thee, Her sins, which are many, are forgiven; for she loved much: but to whom little is forgiven, *the same* loveth little.

48 And he said unto her, Thy sins are forgiven.

John 12:3 Then took Mary a pound of <u>ointment</u> of spikenard, very costly, and <u>anointed</u> the feet of Jesus, and wiped his feet with her hair: and the house was filled with the odour of the <u>ointment</u>.

<u>*My note*</u>: *anoint = set apart*

Luke 4:18 14 And Jesus returned in the power of the Spirit into Galilee: and there went out a fame of him through all the region round about. 15 And he taught in their synagogues, being glorified of all. 16 And he came to Nazareth, where he had been brought up: and, as his custom was, he went into the synagogue on the sabbath day, and stood up for to read. 17 And there was delivered unto him the book of the prophet Esaias. And when he had opened the book, he found the place where it was written, 18 The Spirit of the Lord *is* upon me, because he hath <u>anointed</u> me to preach the gospel to the poor; he hath sent me to heal the brokenhearted, to preach deliverance to the captives, and recovering of sight to the blind, to set at liberty them that are bruised, 19 To preach the acceptable year of the Lord. 20 And he closed the book, and he gave *it* again to the minister, and sat down. And the eyes of all them that were in the synagogue were fastened on him. 21 And he began to say unto them, This day is this scripture fulfilled in your ears.

Acts 10:38 36 The word which *God* sent unto the children of Israel, preaching peace by Jesus Christ: (he is Lord of all:) 37 That word, *I say*, ye know, which was published throughout all Judaea, and began from Galilee, after the baptism which John preached; 38 How <u>God anointed Jesus of Nazareth with the Holy Ghost and with power</u>: who went about doing good, and healing all that were oppressed of the devil; for <u>God was with him</u>.

2Corinthians 1:21 Now he which stablisheth us with you in Christ, and hath <u>anointed</u> us, *is* God; 22 Who hath also sealed us, and given the earnest of the Spirit in our hearts.

<u>*My note*</u>: *anointed = smeared , with clay .*

John 9:6 5 As long as I am in the world, I am the light of the world. 6 When he had thus spoken, he spat on the ground, and <u>made clay of the spittle</u>, and <u>he anointed the eyes of the blind man with the clay</u>, 7 And said unto him, Go, wash in the pool of Siloam, (which is by interpretation, Sent.) He went his way therefore, and washed, and came seeing.

John 9:11 10 Therefore said they unto him, How were thine eyes opened? 11 He answered and said, A man that is called <u>Jesus</u> <u>made clay</u>, and <u>anointed mine eyes</u>, and said unto me, Go to the pool of Siloam, and wash: and I went and washed, and I received sight.

<u>*My note*</u>: *anointed = consecrated with oil*

Leviticus 10:7 And ye shall not go from the door of the tabernacle of the congregation, lest ye die: for <u>the anointing oil of the LORD *is* upon you</u>. And they did according to the words of Moses.

Leviticus 21:10 And *he that is* the high priest among his brethren, <u>upon whose head the anointing oil was poured</u>, and <u>that is consecrated to put on the garments</u>, shall not uncover his head, nor rend his clothes;

Leviticus 21:12 <u>Neither shall he go out of the sanctuary</u>, nor profane the sanctuary of his God; for <u>the crown of the anointing oil of his God *is* upon him</u>: I *am* the LORD.

Ezekiel 16:9 1 Again the word of the LORD came unto me, saying, 2 Son of man, cause Jerusalem to know her abominations,

8 …: yea, I sware unto thee, and entered into a covenant with thee, saith the Lord GOD, and thou becamest mine. 9 Then washed I thee with water; yea, I throughly washed away thy blood from thee, and <u>I anointed thee with oil</u>.

Oil

from: Page 39

Consolation, *n.* **1.** <u>Comfort</u> ; *alleviation of misery, or distress of mind ; refreshment of mind or spirits ; a comparative degree of happiness in distress or misfortune, springing from any circumstances that abates the evil, or supports and strengthens the mind, as hope, joy, courage and the like.*

We have great joy and consolation in thy love. **Philem. 7**

2. *That which comforts, or refreshes the spirits ; the cause of comfort ; as the consolation of Israel.* **Luke ii** .

Luke 2:21 – 39   **25** And behold, there was a man in Jerusalem, whose name *was* Simeon; and the same man *was* just and devout, <u>waiting for the</u> <u>consolation</u> <u>of Israel</u>: and the Holy Ghost was upon him. **26** And it was revealed unto him by the Holy Ghost, that he should not see death, before he had seen the Lord's Christ. **27** And he came by the Spirit into the temple: and when the parents brought in the child <u>Jesus</u>, to do for him after the custom of the law, **28** <u>Then took he him up in his arms, and blessed God</u>, and said, **29** Lord, now lettest thou thy servant depart in peace, according to thy word: **30** <u>For mine eyes have seen thy</u> <u>salvation,</u> **31** Which thou hast prepared before the face of all people; **32** A light to lighten the Gentiles, and the glory of thy people Israel.

Console, *v.t.* [*... The primary sense is either to set or allay, to give rest or quiet, ... or the sense is to strengthen, in which case it coincides with the root of solid. The latter is most probable.*]

<u>To comfort</u> ; *to cheer the mind in distress or depression ; to alleviate grief, and give refreshment to the mind or spirits; to give contentment or moderate happiness by relieving from distress.*

The promises of the gospel may well console the christian in all the afflictions of life.

It is a consoling reflection that the evils of life are temporary.

I am much consoled by the reflection that the religion of Christ has been attacked in vain by all the wits and philosophers, and its triumph has been complete. P. Henry.

Sanctified, *pp.* Made holy ; consecrated ; set apart for sacred services.   2. Affectedly holy.

Sanctify, *v.t.* [..., holy, and ..., to make.]

1. In a general sense, to cleanse,, purify or make holy. Addison.

2. To separate, set apart or appoint to a holy, sacred or religious use.   <u>God blessed the seventh day and sanctified it.</u> **Gen. ii** .
So under the Jewish dispensation, to sanctify the altar, the temple, the priests, & c.

3. To purify ; to prepare for divine service, and for partaking of holy things. **Ex. xix** .

4. To separate, ordain and appoint to the work of redemption and the government of the church. **John x .**

5. To cleanse from corruption ; to purify from sin ; to make holy by detaching the <u>affections</u> from the world and its defilements, and exalting <u>them</u> to a supreme love to God.

Sanctify them through thy truth ; thy word is truth. **John xvii** . **Eph. v** .

6. To make the means of holiness ; to render productive of holiness or piety.
Those judgments of God are the more welcome, as a means which his mercy hath sanctified so to me, as to make me repent of that unjust act. K. Charles .

7. To make free from guilt .   *That holy man, amaz'd at what he saw, Made haste to sanctify the bliss by law. Dryden .*

<u>To sanctify God,</u> <u>to praise and celebrate him as a holy being</u> ; <u>to acknowledge and honor his holy majesty, and to reverence his character and laws</u>.
Is. viii .

<u>God sanctifies himself or his name,</u> <u>by vindicating his honor from the reproaches of the wicked,</u> and <u>manifesting his glory</u>.
Ezek. xxxvi .

Oil

My note: *Jesus was the firstborn of God* : *HE was sanctified unto the LORD GOD, to be the SAVIOUR of the world !!!*

Sanctify   *firstborn*   Exodus 11:1,4,5 ; 12:21-28, 29

Exodus 13:1, 2   1 And the LORD spake unto Moses, saying, 2 Sanctify unto me all the firstborn,
whatsoever openeth the womb among the children of Israel, *both* of man and of beast: it *is* mine.

Exodus 13:12   That thou shalt set apart unto the LORD all that openeth the matrix, and every firstling that cometh
of a beast which thou hast; the males *shall be* the LORD'S.

Exodus 13:15   … ; but all the firstborn of my children I redeem.

Numbers 8:17   For all the firstborn of the children of Israel *are* mine, *both* man and beast:
on the day that I smote every firstborn in the land of Egypt I sanctified them for myself.

Exodus 11:4,5   4 And Moses said, Thus saith the LORD, About midnight will I go out into the midst of Egypt: 5 And all the
firstborn in the land of Egypt shall die, from the firstborn of Pharaoh that sitteth upon the throne, even unto
the firstborn of the maidservant that *is* behind the mill; and all the firstborn of beasts.

Exodus 12:21-29   29 And it came to pass, that at midnight the LORD smote all the firstborn in the land of Egypt,
from the firstborn of Pharaoh that sat on his throne unto the firstborn of the captive that *was* in the dungeon;
and all the firstborn of cattle.

Isaiah

8:13 Sanctify the LORD of hosts himself; and *let* him *be* your fear, and *let* him *be* your dread.

29:23   22 Therefore thus saith the LORD, who redeemed Abraham, concerning the house of Jacob, Jacob shall not now
be ashamed, neither shall his face now wax pale. 23 But when he seeth his children, the work of mine hands,
in the midst of him, they shall sanctify my name, and sanctify the Holy One of Jacob, and shall fear the God of Israel.

66:17 They that sanctify themselves, and purify themselves in the gardens behind one *tree* in the midst, eating swine's flesh,
and the abomination, and the mouse, shall be consumed together, saith the LORD.

Ezekiel

20:12 Moreover also I gave them my sabbaths, to be a sign between me and them,
that they might know that I *am* the LORD that sanctify them.

36:23 And I will sanctify my great name, which was profaned among the heathen, which ye have profaned in the midst of them;
and the heathen shall know that I *am* the LORD, saith the Lord GOD, when I shall be sanctified in you before their eyes.

37:28 And the heathen shall know that I the LORD do sanctify Israel, when my sanctuary shall be in the midst of them
for evermore.

38:23 Thus will I magnify myself, and sanctify myself; and I will be known in the eyes of many nations,
and they shall know that I *am* the LORD.

44:19 And when they go forth into the utter court, *even* into the utter court to the people, they shall put off their garments
wherein they ministered, and lay them in the holy chambers, and they shall put on other garments; and they shall not
sanctify the people with their garments.

John 17:17   Sanctify them through thy truth: thy word is truth.

Ephesians 5:26   That he might sanctify and cleanse it with the washing of water by the word,   27 That he might present it to
himself a glorious church, not having spot, or wrinkle, or any such thing; but that it should be holy and
without blemish.

1Thessalonians 5:23   And the very God of peace sanctify you wholly; and *I pray God* your whole spirit and soul and body be
preserved blameless unto the coming of our Lord Jesus Christ. 24 Faithful *is* he that calleth you,
who also will do *it*.

Hebrews 13:12   Wherefore Jesus also, that he might sanctify the people with his own blood, suffered without the gate.

1Peter 3:15   But sanctify the Lord God in your hearts: and *be* ready always to *give* an answer to every man that asketh you
a reason of the hope that is in you with meekness and fear:

Oil

Sanctifieth

Hebrews
2:11 For both he that sanctifieth and they who are sanctified *are* all of one:

for which cause he is not ashamed to call them brethren,

9:13 For if the blood of bulls and of goats, and the ashes of an heifer sprinkling the unclean, sanctifieth
to the purifying of the flesh: **14** How much more shall the blood of Christ, who through the eternal Spirit
offered himself without spot to God, purge your conscience from dead works to serve the living God?

Sanctified

Genesis 2:3 And God blessed the seventh day, and sanctified it: because that in it he had rested from all his work
which God created and made.

John
17:19 1 These words spake Jesus, and lifted up his eyes to heaven, and said, Father, the hour is come; glorify they Son,
that thy Son also may glorify thee:

16 They are not of the world, even as I am not of the world.
17 Sanctify them through thy truth: thy word is truth.
18 As thou hast sent me into the world, even so have I also sent them into the world.
19 And for their sakes I sanctify myself, that they also might be sanctified through the truth.
20 Neither pray I for these alone, but for them also which shall believe on me through their word;

Acts 26:18 To open their eyes, *and* to turn *them* from darkness to light, and *from* the power of Satan unto God, that they may
Read: 26:14 - 18   receive forgiveness of sins, and inheritance among them which are sanctified by faith that is in me.

Romans 15:16 That I should be the minister of Jesus Christ to the Gentiles, ministering the gospel of God, that the offering up of
the Gentiles might be acceptable, being sanctified by the Holy Ghost.

1Corinthians
1:2 1 Paul, called *to be* an apostle of Jesus Christ through the will of God, and Sosthenes *our* brother, 2 Unto the church of God
which is at Corinth, to them that are sanctified in Christ Jesus, called *to be* saints, with all that in every place call upon
the name of Jesus Christ our Lord, both theirs and ours: 3 Grace *be* unto you, and peace, from God our Father, and
from the Lord Jesus Christ.

6:11 And such were some of you: but ye are washed, but ye are sanctified, but ye are justified in the name of the Lord Jesus,
and by the Spirit of our God.

Hebrews
2:11 For both he that sanctifieth and they who are sanctified *are* all of one:

for which cause he is not ashamed to call them brethren.

10:10 By the which will we are sanctified through the offering of the body of Jesus Christ once *for all*.

10:14 For by one offering he hath perfected for ever them that are sanctified.

10:29 Of how much sorer punishment, suppose ye, shall he be thought worthy, who hath trodden under foot the Son of God, and
hath counted the blood of the covenant, wherewith he was sanctified, an unholy thing, and hath done despite unto
the Spirit of grace?

Jude 1 Jude, the servant of Jesus Christ, and brother of James, to them that are sanctified by God the Father,
and preserved in Jesus Christ, *and* called:

My personal notes:

seal

1Kings 21:8 So she wrote letters in Ahab's name, and <u>sealed *them* with his seal</u>, and sent the letters unto the elders
and to the nobles that *were* in his city, dwelling with Naboth.

Esther
3:12 Then were the king's scribes called on the thirteenth day of the first month, and there was written according to
all that Haman had commanded unto the king's lieutenants, and to the governors that *were* over every
province, and to the rulers of every people of every province according to the writing thereof, and *to* every
people after their language; in the name of king Ahasuerus was it written, <u>and sealed with the king's ring.</u>

8:8,10 **8** Write ye also for the Jews, as it liketh you, in the king's name, <u>and seal *it* with the king's ring</u>:
for the writing which is written in the king's name, and <u>sealed with the king's ring, may no man reverse.</u>

10 And he wrote in the king Ahasuerus' name, and <u>sealed *it* with the king's ring</u>, and sent letters by posts
on horseback, *and* riders on mules, camels, *and* young dromedaries:

Daniel
6:17 And a stone was brought, and laid upon the mouth of the den; and <u>the king sealed it with his own signet,</u>
and with the signet of his lords; that the purpose might not be changed concerning Daniel.
My note: 12:7,8 *man clothed in linen* = <u>he</u>   **Read:** <u>10:5 - 9</u>
12:9 And <u>he</u> said, Go thy way, Daniel: for <u>the words *are* closed up</u> and <u>sealed till the time of the end.</u>

John 6:27 **26** Jesus answered them and said, Verily, verily, I say unto you, Ye seek me, not because ye saw the
miracles, but because ye did eat of the loaves, and were filled. **27** Labour not for the meat which
perisheth, but for that meat which endureth unto everlasting life, which the Son of man shall give
unto you: <u>for him hath God the Father sealed.</u>

2Corinthians 1:21,22 **21** Now he which stablisheth us with you in Christ, and hath anointed us, *is* God;
22 <u>Who hath also sealed us</u>, <u>and given the earnest of the Spirit in our hearts.</u>

Ephesians
1:13,14 **13** In whom ye also *trusted*, after that ye heard the word of truth, the gospel of your salvation: in whom
also after that ye believed, <u>ye were sealed with that holy Spirit of promise</u>, **14** Which is the earnest of our
inheritance until the redemption of the purchased possession, unto the praise of his glory.

Ephesians 4:30 And grieve not the holy Spirit of God, whereby <u>ye are sealed</u> <u>unto the day of redemption.</u>

Revelation 5:1,2,3 **1** And I saw in the right hand of him that sat on the throne a book written within and on the
backside, <u>sealed with seven seals.</u> **2** And I saw a strong angel proclaiming with a loud voice,
<u>Who is worthy to open the book</u>, <u>and to loose the seals thereof</u>? **3** And no man in heaven,
nor in earth, neither under the earth, was able to open the book, neither to look thereon.

Revelation 5:9 **6** And I beheld, and, lo, in the midst of the throne and of the four beasts, and in the midst of the
elders, stood a Lamb as it had been slain, having seven horns and seven eyes, which are the seven
Spirits of God sent forth into all the earth. **7** And he came and took the book out of the right hand
of him that sat upon the throne. **8** And when he had taken the book, the four beasts and four *and*
twenty elders fell down before the Lamb, having every one of them harps, and golden vials full of
odours, which are the prayers of saints. **9** And they sung a new song, saying, <u>Thou art worthy</u>
<u>to take the book</u>, <u>and to open the seals thereof</u>: <u>for thou wast slain</u>, and <u>hast redeemed us to God</u>
<u>by thy blood</u> out of every kindred, and tongue, and people, and nation;

Revelation 6:1 And <u>I saw when the Lamb opened one of the seals</u>, and I heard, as it were the noise of thunder,
one of the four beasts saying, Come and see.

My note: The seals were opened by the Lamb of God: HE is worthy " to loose the seals thereof " " for he is Lord of lords, and King of kings:"*!!!*
Revelation 17:14

Anointed thee with the oil of gladness

Psalm 45:6,7 **6** Thy throne, O God, *is* for ever and ever: the sceptre of thy kingdom *is* a right sceptre.
7 Thou lovest righteousness, and hatest wickedness: therefore God, thy God,
hath <u>anointed thee with the oil of gladness</u> above thy fellows.

Hebrews 1:8,9 **8** But unto the Son he *saith*, Thy throne, O God, *is* for ever and ever: a sceptre of righteousness
is the sceptre of thy kingdom. **9** Thou hath loved righteousness, and hated iniquity; therefore God,
even thy God, hast <u>anointed thee with the oil of gladness</u> above thy fellows.

Even so, come, Lord Jesus. ***Revelation 22:20*** *vs.21* … A-men'.

My personal notes:

Witnessing Scripture

My note: *Every moment in time that Jesus does not return, is an opportunity for someone to repent and to receive HIM, as one's own personal Lord & Saviour; becoming a child of God, now and shall be with HIM, for ever!*

2Peter 3:9   The Lord is not slack concerning his promise, as some men count slackness;
Read: all of Ch. 3   but is longsuffering to us-ward, not willing that any should perish,
but that all should come to repentance.

God Loves You

For God so loved the world, that he gave his only begotten Son, that whosoever believeth in him
should not perish, but have everlasting life.   **John 3:16**

For God sent not his Son into the world to condemn the world;
but that the world through him might be saved.   **John 3:17**

But God commendeth his love toward us, in that, while we were yet sinners, Christ died for us.
Romans 5:8

All are sinners

As it is written, There is none righteous, no, not one: **Romans 3:10**

For all have sinned, and come short of the glory of God;   **Romans 3:23**

God's remedy for sin

For the wages of sin *is* death; but the gift of God *is* eternal life through Jesus Christ our Lord.
Romans 6:23

But as many as received him, to them gave he power to become the sons of God,
even to them that believe on his name: **John 1:12**

3 For I delivered unto you first of all that which I also received, how that Christ died for our sins
according to the scriptures; 4 And that he was buried, and that he rose again the third day
according to the scriptures: **1Corinthians 15:3,4**

All may be saved now

Behold, I stand at the door, and knock: if any man hear my voice, and open the door,
I will come in to him, and will sup with him, and he with me.   **Revelation 3:20**

For whosoever shall call upon the name of the Lord shall be saved. **Romans 10:13**

Assurance as a believer

That if thou shalt confess with thy mouth the Lord Jesus, and shalt believe in thine heart that God
hath raised him from the dead, thou shalt be saved.   **Romans 10:9**

Verily, verily, I say unto you, He that heareth my word, and believeth on him that sent me,
hath everlasting life, and shall not come into condemnation; but is passed from death unto life.   **John 5:24**

But these are written, that ye might believe that Jesus is the Christ, the Son of God;
and that believing ye might have life through his name.   **John 20:31**

I love you Lord

prayer

I love you Lord, because you first loved me;

and you gave yourself for me Lord;

a ransom, for me;

removing my sins from the eyes of the Holiness of God!

Lord, you paid my sin debt in full;

Thank you!

Lord, in you I have life, and I have life more abundantly!

Lord, I rest in you, now and for ever!

Even so, come, Lord Jesus.   *Revelation 22:20*   *vs.21*... A-men'.

My Personal Notes:

My Personal Notes:

My Personal Notes:

My Personal Notes:

THE HOLY SPIRIT of God

The Holy Bible *The KingJamesVersion*

The New Strong's Exhaustive Concordance of the Bible   *KingJamesVersion*

An American Dictionary of the English Language Noah Webster 1828

All Scripture is recorded from:

The Holy Bible *The KingJamesVersion*

God's holy word recorded in the English language.

Referencing was with the aid of:

The New Strong's Exhaustive Concordance of the Bible *KingJamesVersion*

This concordance was, and is, a continual aid to me in taking the truth of the Lord, which is set before me of the Holy Spirit and receiving a confirmation from the Lord, where a peace comes upon me; The peace of knowing that what was set before me was complete and is made manifest within HIS Holy Word; according to the truth in which it was given within Scripture.

All word definitions are recorded from:

An American Dictionary of the English Language Noah Webster 1828

My note: There are three quotes in the beginning preface of this dictionary which are referenced as being quoted by Noah Webster; *"If the foundation be destroyed, what can the righteous do?"* **Psalm 11:3**

and

"In my view, the Christian religion is the *most important and one of the first things* in which *all* children, under a free government, ought to be instructed. … No truth is more evident to my mind than that the Christian religion must be the basis of any government intended to secure the rights and privileges of a free people. …"

and

"An immense effect may be produced by small powers wisely and steadily directed." Noah Webster, 1821.

Noah Webster

Oct. 16, 1758 Born

May 28, 1843 Died ; passing on from this life at age 84

Also,

1776 he would have been 18 yrs. old

1807 his testimony of receiving Jesus Christ as his personal Lord & Saviour, at the age of 49

1828 he would have been 70 yrs. old   American Dictionary of the English Language Noah Webster 1828

The *American Dictionary of the English Language Noah Webster 1828*, has numerous references from the *KingJamesVersion of* **The Holy Bible**; with many verses noted and quoted. This has been a blessing to me as I have recorded what my Lord has set before me. When I read and consider the meaning of a word as is defined and recorded by Noah Webster, a truth of the Word of the Lord unfolds and becomes a confirmation from the Holy Spirit of many truths within God's holy word.

What a glorious peace in knowing the truth of God's holy word when declaring HIS word to others, by the leading of the Holy Spirit; lifting up my Lord & my Saviour Jesus Christ, who is the Saviour of the World !!!

www.ingramcontent.com/pod-product-compliance
Lightning Source LLC
Chambersburg PA
CBHW041514120626
46551CB00018B/2431